Jesus in the Eyes of His Followers

The Dead Sea Scrolls &
Christian Origins Library
4

Jesus in the Eyes of His Followers

Newly Discovered Manuscripts and Old Christian Confessions

by
Petr Pokorný

BIBAL Press
North Richland Hills, Texas

BIBAL Press
An imprint of D. & F. Scott Publishing, Inc.
P.O. Box 821653
N. Richland Hills, TX 76182
1-888-788-2280
bibal@cmpu.net
www.cmpu.net/public/bibal

Printed in the United States of America

02 01 00 99 98 5 4 3 2 1

Library of Congress Cataloging-in-Publication Data

Pokorny, Petr.
  Jesus in the eyes of His followers : newly discovered manuscripts and old Christian confessions / by Petr Pokorny.
    p. cm. -- (The Dead Sea scrolls & Christian origins library ; 4)
  Includes bibliographical references.
  ISBN 0-94-103765-7
  1. Jesus Christ--History of doctrines--Early church, ca. 30-600.
  2. Bible. N.T.--Criticism, interpretation, etc. I. Title. II. Series.
  BT198 .P62 1998
  232'.09'015--ddc21
                                        98-25310
                                         CIP

Images not otherwise credited are courtesy of www.arttoday.com
Cover by KC Scott

Contents

Publisher's Preface

BIBAL Press is pleased to publish The Dead Sea Scrolls & Christian Origins Library under the general editorship of Prof. James H. Charlesworth, a distinguished scholar who is the George L. Collord Professor of New Testament Language and Literature at Princeton Theological Seminary and the editor of the Dead Sea Scrolls Project at Princeton Theological Seminary. Among his many other accomplishments, he has been involved in the discovery of more than four thousand biblical and religious manuscripts.

This series was undertaken for the purpose of presenting the general public with the best and latest information regarding the numerous ancient manuscripts which have come to light during the last half century, with the current state of biblical archaeology, and with the impact that these are having on our understanding of Early Christianity and First-Century Judaism. Each volume is written by one of the world's leading experts on its subject matter—all of them scholars who are actually working with the manuscripts or archaeological sites which are discussed.

It is our goal to make this information readily available even to those who may have little or no knowledge of the subject matter. Accordingly, we have avoided technical jargon as much as possible and have provided a glossary explaining terms which may not be familiar to all readers. The first appearance in the book of each word explained in the glossary is presented in bold typeface. We have included endnotes, which are not necessary to understanding the text. These simply provide technical information and references which are helpful to scholars and students who are also finding these little volumes a useful addition to their libraries.

We hope that you enjoy this privileged peek into the arena of world-class scholarship on some of the most fascinating developments in the history of biblical studies.

W. R. Scott

Editor's Preface

Volume 4 in The Dead Sea Scrolls & Christian Origins Library presents the insights of Professor Petr Pokorný. An internationally recognized leader in the attempt to clarify the origins of Christianity, he has held the New Testament chair at Charles University in Prague for decades. Although he has been celebrated as perhaps the most gifted and perceptive biblical scholar specializing in Christian Origins in the East, most of his publications have been inaccessible to English readers because they are written in Czech or German. The publication of this volume is thus a special honor.

Pokorný has made several significant contributions to a better understanding of the origins of Christianity and of Christology. He has helped clarify that the New Testament canon was not shaped by a council decision, but evolved over the first four centuries. These insights were published in *Literární a teologický úvod do Nového zákona* (1993). In *Píseň o perle* (1986), *Řecké dědictví v Orientu* (1993), and *Tomášovo evangelium* (1981), he showed that Gnosticism must not be branded as heretical and that it began as gnosis before the end of the first century CE. His focus was on one of the most beautiful poetic compositions of very early Gnosticism (or proto-Gnosticism), *The Hymn of the Pearl*. He also correctly pointed out the similarity of *The Hymn of the Pearl* to the *Odes of Solomon* and the *Gospel of Thomas*.

His *Die Entstehung der Christologie* (1985) was translated into English in 1987 with the title *The Genesis of Christology*. On the basis of this and similar research, he offered his opinion regarding the future of Christian belief in a work entitled *Die Zukunft des Glaubens* (1992). The next millennium will surely see success for the Christian Church if its leaders are as careful and as forthright as Pokorný has been with the truth about the beginnings of Christian faith.

J. H. Charlesworth
Institutum Iudaicum
Tübingen, July 1998

Acknowledgments

I would like to express my sincere thanks to my old friend, Prof. James H. Charlesworth, to the editor, Dr. William R. Scott, and to my assistant, Mrs. Lucy Kopecka, who by various means promoted the genesis of this book.

Petr Pokorný

Abbreviations

§ — Refers to numbered sections of this book

AGJU — Arbeiten zur Geschichte des antiken Judentums und des Urchristentums

AncB Ref Lib — Anchor Bible Reference Library

ANRW — Aufstieg und Niedergang der römischen Welt

BCE — Before the Common Era (= BC)

BHT — Beiträge zur historischen Theologie

BZNW — Beihefte zur *Zeitschrift für die neutestamentliche Wissenschaft*

CD — *Damascus Document*

CE — Common Era (= AD)

Did — *Didache*

ExpTim — *Expository Times*

EvT — *Evangelische Theologie*

frgm. — Fragment

FRLANT — Forschungen zur Religion und Literatur des Alten und Neuen Testaments

FS — Festschrift

GosPhil — *Gospel of Philip*

GosThom — *Gospel of Thomas*

Gr. — Greek

HKNT Supl — Handcommentar zum Neuen Testament (supplement)

JBL — *Journal of Biblical Literature*

Jos bell — Josephus Flavius, *Bellum Iudaicum*

JSNTSup — Journal for the Study of the New Testament—Supplement Series

JSPSup — Journal for the Study of the Pseudepigrapha—Supplement Series

Log. — *Logion*, saying

LXX — Septuagint

NRSV — New Revised Standard Version

NTS — *New Testament Studies*

NHC — Nag Hammadi Codex

NHS — Nag Hammadi Studies

NTTS — New Testament Tools and Studies

RSV — Revised Standard Version

SBLMS — SBL Monograph Series

SBT — Studies in Biblical Theology

SibOr — *Sibylline Oracles*

Sir — Sirach

SNTSMS — Society for New Testament Studies Monograph Series

Syr Bar — Syriac (2nd) *Apocalypse of Baruch*

THNT — Theologischer Handkommentar zum Neuen Testament

TRE — Theologische Realenzyklopaedie

Trim. Prot. — *Trimorphic Protennoia*

TSAJ — Text und Studien zum antiken Judentum

UTB — Uni-Taschenbücher

WUNT — Wissenschaftliche Untersuchungen zum Neuen Testament

The Problem

1.1 What is Christology?

The simplest answer to this question is that Christology is a reflected expression of Jesus' significance. This does not necessarily include the idea that Jesus of Nazareth is the incarnation of God himself, the Son of God in terms of later ecclesiastical teaching on the trinity; however, in all Christologies, Jesus is the one who opened the way toward God himself.

New Testament Christology is the set of expressions of Jesus' significance (Christologies) as we find them in the text of the New Testament.

Christology always includes a witness, proclamation, or message (about something related to the human world) and an evaluation. There are in ancient literature various speculative concepts of human salvation and undeveloped messages about individuals with messianic ambitions. However, only indirectly may we call these Christology. And since every reflection is directed at a better orientation in the human world, Christology always includes elements of some kind of philosophy.

Unlike other evaluations of somebody's significance, Christology always deals with Jesus' positive and absolute, final, eschatological or soteriological significance. The expression "Christology" as a technical term originates in post-New Testament Christian theology.

The last principal feature of any Christology is obvious from the etymology: Christo-logy is a teaching about the Anointed One (in Greek *christos*, in Hebrew *māšiach* = Messiah). For an ordinary Greek, *christos* as a title was as incomprehensible as it is for non-Christians in contemporary English. However, in

1

Hebrew or Aramaic it was a fixed and well-known title for an expected key person, at least among some groups of the Jewish population both in Palestine and the **diaspora**. This does not apply only to the title *christos*; all Christologies are in some respect related to Jewish expectations or to the text of the Jewish Bible (Tanakh, Scripture)—the Christian Old Testament. In some christological concepts, this relation may be only a secondary or marginal phenomenon. Nevertheless, none of the early Christologies can deny that its roots are in Jewish soil.

1.2 The Formula of Faith—1 Cor 15:3b–5

A Sample of one of the Christologies or a Focal Point of a Development toward Christological Integration?

The text we shall discuss at the very beginning—a text of crucial importance—serves as a good illustration of our definition of Christology in addition to being the starting point of our discussion of the problem. Below are verses 1–14, so that you can see this passage in its context, something which we should have always in sight when interpreting the Formula of Faith:

> (1) Now, brothers, I would remind you of the gospel (Greek *euaggelion*) that I proclaimed to you, which you received (*parelabete*) and in which you stand, (2) through which you are saved, if you hold firmly to the word through which I proclaimed it to you—unless you believed in vain. (3) For I passed on (*paredoka*) to you as of first importance what I also received (*parelabon*):
>
> that Christ died for our sins according to the Scriptures, (4) that he was buried, that he was raised on the third day according to the Scriptures, (5) and that he appeared to Cephas and to the Twelve.
>
> (6) After that, he appeared to more than five hundred brothers at the same time, most of whom are still living, though some have fallen asleep. (7) Then he appeared to James, then to all the apostles. (8) Last of all as to one abnormally born, he appeared also to me. (9) For I am the least of the apostles, not deserving to be called an apostle, because I persecuted the church of God. (10) But by the grace of God I am what I am, and his grace toward me was not without effect. On the contrary, I worked harder than any of them, though it was not I, but the grace of God

which was with me. (11) Whether, then, it was I or they, this is what we preach, and this is what you believed.

(12) Now since Christ is proclaimed as raised from the dead, how can some of you say that there is no resurrection of the dead? (13) If there is no resurrection of the dead, then not even Christ has been raised. (14) And if Christ has not been raised, then our proclamation is in vain and your faith is in vain. (1 Cor 15:1–14)

1.2.1 The Date and Extent of the Formula

The Formula of Faith in 1 Cor 15:3b–5 is an extraordinary witness. Since it is quoted in the oldest set of texts of Christian literature, the authentic Pauline letters, it is obviously a part of an older tradition, three of its links to the past being explicitly mentioned: "received," "passed on," and again "received" (15:1–3). Since the epistles to the Corinthians were written in the 50s CE, Paul must have learned the formula at the latest in Antioch. It is even possible that he learned it in Jerusalem. If the latter assumption were true, the formula could be a translation from Aramaic. Unfortunately, the lack of evidence prevents us from giving any definitive answer. At any rate, even if the formula originated in Antioch and Paul learned it in the 40s, it is an extraordinary early witness. It is certain that there are various older traditions and that we may deduce an indirect Christology from traditions about the life of Jesus, but their dating is always controversial. Thus, this formula is extraordinarily valuable as a solid basis for our discussion, since it is—as we shall see—a pre-Pauline cluster of explicit christological utterances which have been set in their form by **liturgical** usage and bound together by a sophisticated structure, the shaping and stabilizing of which must have taken several years. The rough shape of the Formula of Faith was most probably finished not later than the mid-40s, not more than fifteen years after the crucifixion of Jesus.

However, it would be an illusion to suppose that the older a text is, the more important is the Christology it represents. At the beginning of the Christian church, the movement of Jesus' followers most probably started in many independent groups and only gradually did it coalesce into a church with a more or less standard teaching. Some of the early expressions of faith in

Jesus Christ remained on the periphery and disappeared without being suppressed simply because they were very inadequate and the people who used them soon recognized that the other confessions were better expressions of their faith. In sum, the Formula of Faith is significant not because of its early origin alone; it is the combination of the early origin, the complexity of the formula, and its success in the Church that gives it weight.

When discussing the Formula of Faith, we ought to mention that there are some problems with determining exactly where it ends. Paul clearly indicates its beginning by the Greek word *hoti* ("that") in verse 3, which in practice functioned like our modern colon. However, the end of the quotation, i.e., the end of the gospel as he proclaimed it in Corinth, is not indicated. Undoubtedly, verse 8, where Paul mentioned himself, did not belong to it. This does not, however, mean that the rest of the list of the immediate receivers of the post-Easter appearances of Jesus belongs to the original formula. Verses 5–7 obviously list the persons who "this proclaim," i.e., who preach the gospel on the basis of this formula, so that they were not necessarily a part of the formula themselves. On the other hand, it is unlikely that the formula includes none of the names. As we shall see, its content is fourfold. Christ:

(a) died
    (b) was buried
(c) was raised
    (d) appeared.

The units (b) and (d) confirm the authenticity of (a) and (c). And since the appearances have to be attested (otherwise the claim would be meaningless), at least the first group of witnesses—Cephas (Peter) and the Twelve—must have belonged to the formula. In fact, at the time of the appearances, Judas was dead, so that the receivers of the second appearance could have been only *eleven* people, but, since according to the **synoptic** tradition *twelve* was a term for the group of Jesus' disciples who symbolized the twelve tribes of the renewed people of God, the formulation is meaningful and theologically important. Peter, as the first witness of the resurrection, is attested in a narrative way by both the synoptic Gospels and the Johannine literature (see §1.2.8), so that most **exegetes** consider verses 3b–5 to be the Formula of Faith ("this is what you believed"—v. 11).

This can be confirmed by comparison with the last verses of the Gospel of Mark (in the oldest manuscripts Mark ended with 16:8), where in the place where the crucified Jesus was laid (16:6), the messenger of God dressed in a white robe proclaims that Jesus has risen and sends the women to tell the news to the disciples and Peter (16:7). This narrative reveals knowledge of the Formula of Faith or of a tradition related to it and tries to harmonize it with the story of the women at the tomb, which is attested only here, several decades after the formula was created. We will discuss the role of the formula in shaping the written Gospels in §3.4.2, but, from what we have observed so far, we can confirm only that the formula is identical with 1 Cor 15:3b–5.

1.2.2 The Positive Meaning

The formula is called "good news" (the *gospel*—in Old English god spel = "good news"— in Greek *euaggelion*, v. 1). This is a typically Christian signal of its positive content. Originally, *euaggelion* was the reward for the messenger of good news, later the good news itself. However, only in the Greek Bible (the Septuagint)—the Bible favored by early Christians—where *euaggelion* was used as a translation of the Hebrew *běśorâ* (originally "news" in a neutral sense), did it achieve the meaning "good news" (especially in Isa 40:9; 41:27; cf. 60:6; 61:1; Ps 96:2; 1 Chr 16:23). Thus, this term had important emotional and religious overtones which emphasized the positive nature of the proclamation for many Christian groups, particularly those which considered their proclamation as witnessing the resurrection of Jesus (1 Cor 15:4, 12; 1 Thess 1:10; Rom 1:4, etc.). In fact, the term *euaggelion* became so attractive that the Christians started using it also as a designation of a typically Christian literary subgenre—of the gospel as book, as a biography of Jesus.

1.2.3 Resurrection and Exaltation

As we have just mentioned, the content of the good news, of the gospel, is that Christ "was raised" (1 Cor 15:4 or Mark 16:6, etc.). The passive voice is used in order that the name of God may be avoided, as was common in Jewish practice (to prevent trespassing the second commandment). That God raised Jesus is explicitly proclaimed in verse 15. As we have seen when discussing the term *euaggelion,* the sentence "Christ was raised"—in fact, a short story—was the backbone of all Christian proclamation, not only in this formula, but also for Paul and for most of the Christian texts that were later canonized by the Church.

It is typical of the Jewish-Christian culture that the narrative which expresses God's character is related to history. God is the one who raised Jesus (from death), or (in the Christian Old Testament) God is the one who brought (Israel) out of the land of Egypt, the house of bondage (Exod 20:2).

What does the resurrection mean? In fact, it is a metaphor, since "to raise" means just to wake up, to stand up, to recover one's wits. So it is also with the Greek equivalent and with the Hebrew verb *qûm* which was its Hebrew and Aramaic counterpart (we can deduce from Mark 5:41). At the beginning, the metaphor seems to be used without any additional comment (i.e., without pointing out that it was raising from death). This means that the resurrection was a part of some image or expectation commonly known by the addressees of the Early Christian proclamation.

The first images of resurrection are to be found in the intertestamental **apocalyptic** literature (4 Ezra 7:32–35; *1 Enoch* 51:1ff; cf. 2 Macc 6:18 – 7:12). Resurrection signaled the opening of the new age; it was the link between the present age and the coming one; and the apocalyptic expectations illustrate how the message about Jesus' resurrection became good news for other people and not only a happy ending for his own story. Thus, the apocalyptic expectation served as a means of expressing the general significance of Jesus, and apocalypticism became the mother of Christian theology (Ernst Käsemann). This was virtually a consensus of exegetes during the 1960s and 1970s.

However, the apocalyptic interpretation of the good news also created serious problems. The proclamation of Jesus' resurrection evoked an enthusiastic expectation of the near end of this age and a second coming of Christ in glory. The theology of almost all of the books of the New Testament can be seen coping with this dangerous element of early Christian piety.

However, there seems to be more at work here than just Jewish apocalypticism. The Greek concept *apotheōsis*—the elevation of a person to godhood—or at least a concept of an individual resurrection as a sign (cf. Rev 11:7–13), played a more important role in shaping early Christology than is commonly recognized. In the Qumran hymnic fragment from cave four[1] the righteous one proclaims "I shall be reckoned with gods." This is very similar to Jesus' ascension to heaven according to Luke.[2] We do not know the full context of this fragment. However, the exaltation seems not to be principally associated with an apocalyptic coming of the New Age—it is not opening the comprehensive future hope.

So, the current scholarly consensus may be summarized as follows:

(a) The expected apocalyptic resurrection included also the element of exaltation—of an exaltation to the level of angels (*1 Enoch* 51, cf. Luke 20:36), so that Jesus' resurrection and exaltation were interchangeable in the earliest Christian texts (e.g., Phil 2:9—"God has highly exalted him"), and in non-Jewish settings, where apocalyptic imagery was unknown, the exaltation served as an interpretation of the gospel on Jesus' resurrection.

(b) Unlike the stories about apotheosis or about individual raising from death, in the tradition of the resurrection/exaltation of Jesus his exaltation includes always his personal key position. His "above" is the absolute above: "(He was) designated Son of God in power . . . by his resurrection from the dead" (Rom 1:4); "God has highly exalted him" (Phil 2:9); "that in everything he may be preeminent" (Col 1:18b); "(God) will judge the world with justice by a man whom he has appointed, and of this he has given assurance to all men by raising him from the dead" (Acts 17:31). In other words, the resurrection/exaltation of Jesus not only implies his own rehabilitation, but applies to all the world (to all creation), to all humankind.

(c) An almost self-evident, commonly accepted observation is that the good news about the resurrection and/or exaltation of Jesus appears mostly separated from the other important narrative expression of Jesus' significance that we find in the

Formula of Faith—the Christology of Jesus' sacrificial death. In the following passage, in 1 Cor 15:12, we have an evidence of it, and many other occurrences support this conclusion. This means that both elements are independent expressions of Jesus' significance and that the Formula of Faith is a combination of several christological expressions and traditions, a synthetic, complex text. This observation has important consequences not only for discussion of the beginnings of Christology and the function of the so-called Easter events, but also for their chronology. The proclamation of Jesus' resurrection/exaltation must have been a typical feature of several Christian groups before it was included in the complex Formula of Faith, i.e., earlier than the 40s and very soon after Jesus' death.

1.2.4 The Substitutive Death

". . . Christ died for our sins" is the other christological sentence included in the Formula of Faith (1 Cor 15:3b). According to it, the death of Jesus is not his own tragedy, it is not a defeat in any sense. It is a death which in its consequences helps other people in a decisive way. In this broader sense, it was a substitute death already according to the tradition of the Eucharist (Lord's Supper), as it is preserved in Mark 14:22–25 and in 1 Cor 11:23–25.

This is the element which indirectly motivated interest in the earthly Jesus and possibly influenced the structure of the literary Gospels.

1.2.5 The Combination of Two Narrative Christologies

The Formula of Faith combines the sentence about the substitutive death and the good news about resurrection. Their mutual relation is given by the sequence of the narrative. The Formula of Faith is an early, pre-Pauline evidence of the combination of these two "narrative" Christologies. Paul supported this connection theologically in 2 Cor 5:14–15; Rom 4:24–25; 6:1–11; 8:31–34, etc., and in this way he contributed to the victory of this death and resurrection Christology and helped to create the classical teaching of the Church. The backbone of all the later ecumenical confessions, such as the Apostolic Creed or the Nicaeno-Constantinopolitan Creed, is present here in a preliminary form. The combination of Jesus' cross, his resurrection, and his post-Easter appearances started the development of a Christology expressed through a narrative. It is an elementary and short narrative which nevertheless could be called a Christian **myth**: a story spanning the distance between heavens and earth. The preexistence is not expressly proclaimed, but the phrase "according to the Scriptures" clearly hints at the transcendental frame of the story as whole, which later developed into a Christian "Redeemer Myth" and influenced also the structure of the literary Gospels.

⚘ Excursus on the Function of Myths

In this context, the term "myth" has not any deprecatory meaning (see §1.3.2). Myths expressed the context of human life. They were attempts to put human experience into a wider frame, and their intention was not to create an evidenced worldview. Myths were, rather, interpretative texts; they functioned as models, helping to get an orientation in life and in history. They were not totally exclusive, so that in the New Testament we may meet several versions of the Christian myth (cf. e.g., Revelation 12). As we shall see (§3.3.2.1), the Nag Hammadi texts evoked a new discussion about the role of the Gnostic mythical scheme in the formulation of some early Christian confessional statements about Jesus (e.g., Phil 2:6–11 or Col 1:15–20; cf. Eph 2:14–17a). The suggested new model of understanding the developments of Christology has not been generally accepted, yet the discussion changed the alternatives and helped to understand better the interrelation of the earliest christological statements.

Unlike other myths, the Christian Redeemer Myth stressed the role played by a concrete person of history and, as we have already mentioned, in mainstream Christianity rather evoked than suppressed an interest in Jesus' pre-Easter life and teaching.

1.2.6 Christological Titles

In Rom 10:9, Paul quotes a rule which tries to define the mutual relation of two varied rhetorics expressing the significance of Jesus—the narrative gospel and the christological titles: ". . . if you confess with your mouth *Jesus is the Lord* and believe in your heart that *God raised him from the dead*, you will be saved." The acclamation of Jesus as the Lord was the liturgical expression of faith in his real presence as the Risen One—in his key position for human lives and for history.

In 1 Corinthians 15, we find the title Lord (*kyrios*) in verse 57 only, but *christos* (Heb. *māšiach*), i.e., "the Anointed One," is the title used in the formula itself (v. 3b). Since it appears without an article, as a name, many exegetes have supposed that this is an argument for a later origin of the formula. In Paul's writings, the word *Christ* often has the function of a name (e.g., 1 Cor 15:57). *Christos* is often used with an article as a title (e.g., 1 Cor 15:22). However, *christos* appears without an article as a title, too. John 4:25 is convincing evidence of this.

So the titles and narrative testimonies of faith are two rhetorically different means of Christology. In 1 Cor 15:28, we read about the Son, which is a narrative hint at the title "Son of God." These few instances are possibly good enough to demonstrate the role of the titles of Jesus in early Christianity so that the reader may understand why scholars like Vincent Taylor or Oscar Cullmann tried to reconstruct early Christology through investigation of the titles.

As to the title Christos = Messiah, the formula is in fact a comment on it explaining the nature of the true Messiah. In the next chapter (§2.3), we shall discuss the role of a possible Messianic self-understanding of Jesus in the context of the contemporary Messianic expectations as we can deduce them from the (partially newly discovered) Jewish literature from the time of the Hellenistic and Roman rule in Palestine. It is clear from the very beginning that the portrait of the Messiah (Christ) as it is painted here differs from the Jewish expectations. In any case, the title *christos* is a signal of the soteriological and eschatological impact of Jesus.

1.2.7 According to the Scriptures

The phrase "according to the Scriptures," which appears twice in the formula (verses 3b and 4b), declares the attested story to be an expression of God's will as it is evidenced in the Bible. "Scriptures" means the Jewish Bible—the Law and the Prophets (and Psalms; see Luke 24:44). Since the first Christian generation were Jews, the phrase "according to the Scriptures" should legitimize the Formula of Faith as the fulfillment of all the biblical promises and expectations. The first impression for non-Christian Jews must have been that of provocation, since, in fact, most of the individual passages which are mentioned are by no means typical of the whole of the Scriptures. For the substitute sacrifice in 3b it is in Isa 53:4 where we may read about the Servant of the Lord—a collective Messianic figure—that he took up our infirmities and carried our sorrows. For the resurrection on the third day, we have the more problematic passage from Hos 6:2 on the expected divine help coming on the third day, which is criticized by God himself in Hos 6:4ff.

The first consequence of the fact that it is so difficult to find explicit evidence for any of the appearances of the phrase "according to the Scriptures" is that these are expressions of a more general conviction about Jesus as the culminating event of the Jewish pilgrimage through history as it is attested in the Bible. According to 1 Cor 10:11, the Scriptures serve as exhortation for Christians who (after Easter) live in the time of the fulfillment of the ages. So Jesus is considered to be the apex and fulfillment of God's revelation in history, as *the* revelation, as it is proclaimed in Heb 1:1–2: "In the past God spoke to our ancestors through the prophets in many and various ways, but in these last days he has spoken to us through his Son, whom he appointed heir of all things . . ."

The second consequence of the difficulties encountered in the search for the explicit biblical background of the formula is that the conviction that it must have happened according to the Scriptures resulted from an additional attempt at its interpretation.

Third, we may deduce that the phrase "according to the Scriptures" originally functioned as a legitimization of the gospel in its original Jewish setting.

However, more important is the fourth consequence: Already in the time of apostle Paul, the phrase "according to the Scriptures" actually functioned to support the authority of the Jewish Bible—the Scriptures—in congregations consisting mostly of Christians of pagan origin. Thus, the formula contributed to the later canonization of Scripture by the majority of Christians (§3.5). The risen Lord opens the Scriptures (Luke

24:32) and so the Church decided to adopt what was attested in the Scriptures for its own past.

1.2.8 The Appearances

In §1.2.1 we have already given the reasons why the appearances to the first set of witnesses (verse 5) belong to the original pre-Pauline formula. The Greek word *ophthē* (appeared) means that Jesus was seen by Peter and by the Twelve in a new, elevated status, and that they did not meet him on their own initiative, but that he became visible on his own, or God's initiative. At least, so they interpreted what happened to them soon after the attested resurrection. This means, in fact, that there is no other access to the reality of resurrection than through the testimony of those who experienced Jesus' first appearances.

On the other hand, the appearances, in spite of all the differences in Jesus' status, include a confirmation of his identity. It was Jesus whom they recognized as Christ. As for our interpretation of the phenomenon which is called "appearances," it was obviously possible to experience and to interpret it also in ways which were quite different from what is expressed by the resurrection/exaltation Christology. As we shall see in §3.1.3–4 and §3.3.2.1, some texts from Nag Hammadi speak of an alternative Christology.

As for Peter, we have multiple evidence about his special role in the beginning of the post-Easter Christian proclamation (1 Cor 15:5; Luke 24:34; cf. Mark 16:7; John 20:6–8). He most probably was the first who proclaimed the risen Lord. Or to put it another way, he was the first who called his Easter experience "resurrection" and who started to proclaim it as the gospel.

1.2.9 The List of Witnesses

The list of those who were witnesses of Jesus' appearances includes a special large group of his adherents (five hundred of the brothers, verse 6), some of whom had already died. This is obviously an additional comment by Paul, revealing the intent of his argument in 1 Corinthians 15. A group of members of the Corinthian Christian community denied the hope of resurrection for individual Christians (v. 12). They obviously did not deny the resurrection of Jesus Christ (see verse 12, etc.). The quotation of the formula serves also as a rather awkward argument against their position. However, in spite of this comment, we still may recognize the logic of Paul's argument: How could we continue to proclaim the Lord's resurrection if those whom he dignified as witnesses of his resurrection would die without any hope? We shall discuss the possible intent of the non-resurrection party later (§1.2.10).

James (v. 7a) is the brother of Jesus (Gal 1:19), and the apostles are another group of Christian missionaries than the Twelve.

The last of all is Paul himself. He admits his inferior status resulting from the temporal distance between the appearances to Peter and the appearance to him. However, he considers himself an apostle and often stresses this in answer to those who doubt his apostolic authority (Galatians 1).

It is very probable that Paul, when teaching the formula, informed the Galatians about the list of its warrantors, too. Such a list would function as a demonstration of the ecumenical unity of several groups in early Christianity. The listed groups and individuals are those who must have agreed to call their Easter experience by terms (gospel), images (Jesus' death as sacrifice), and categories (the apocalyptic resurrection) which were used in the Formula of Faith.[3]

However, Paul used the list with a second intention, too. The fact that he stressed that he was the last one of the apostles means that there are no apostles after him. It follows that those who preach and teach the wisdom of the risen Lord (cf. 1 Cor 1:22) and are not in accordance with the formula are not authentic apostles. The authentic apostles are those listed above, Paul being the last witness of Jesus' appearances. It is obvious that those who denied the hope of resurrection do not belong to the authoritative group, nor do any who were presenting any other new teachings allegedly derived from their direct contact with the risen Lord.

1.2.10 Other Christologies

At this point, we encounter a serious problem of Early Christian Christologies. In 1 Cor 15, Paul quotes the Formula of Faith in order to refute a false teaching which, as we have mentioned, in his interpretation, is a denial of the hope of resurrection (see §3.2.2).

This means that the Christologies which were integrated in the formula, as influential as they may have been, by no means represented the only Christian teaching. As early as the 1930s, Walter Bauer warned against the anachronistic transposing of contemporary norms of Christianity (Jesus' substitutive death and the hope linked with his resurrection) into the first century. The other groups soon disappeared in the shadow of the great Church that gradually created a global ecclesiastical structure. Traces of them may be found in newly discovered documents, and it is our intention to investigate the full spectrum of Early Christian Christologies, as far as we may reconstruct them, to discuss the reasons why the resurrection/exaltation Christology attained the leading position, and to discover why some Christologies were integrated and others excluded.

1.3 History of Research

1.3.1 The Ecclesiastical Christology
In the period between the Jewish War and the end of the first century, the Christology of the Formula of Faith became the backbone of the literary Gospels, which subsequently shaped almost all ecclesiastical liturgy and teaching.

1.3.2 From Reimarus to Albert Schweitzer
In the eighteenth century, the German scholar Hermann S. Reimarus (1694–1768) wrote his programmatic essay "On the Purpose of Jesus and His Disciples,"[4] which was an attempt to destroy the "Redeemer Myth" (see §1.2.5). In the name of deistic rationalism, he intended to purify the faith in God and accused the apostles of creating a new religious system which is contrary to the intent of Jesus as teacher and prophet.

His elimination of Easter is understandable from the point of view of historical evidence. We have no access to Easter (resurrection, exaltation, rehabilitation of Jesus, appearances) other than through the testimonies of the apostles. Unfortunately, Reimarus's pioneering work in historical criticism was not balanced by a wise interpretation. The lack of any historical quotation of the formula serves also as a rather awkward argument against their position. However, in spite of this comment, we still may recognize the logic of Paul's argument: How could we continue to proclaim the Lord's resurrection if those whom he dignified as witnesses of his resurrection would die without any hope? We shall discuss the possible intent of the non-resurrection party later (§1.2.10).

James (v. 7a) is the brother of Jesus (Gal 1:19), and the apostles are another group of Christian missionaries than the Twelve.

The last of all is Paul himself. He admits his inferior status resulting from the temporal distance between the appearances to Peter and the appearance to him. However, he considers himself an apostle and often stresses this in answer to those who doubt his apostolic authority (Galatians 1).

It is very probable that Paul, when teaching the formula, informed the Galatians about the list of its warrantors, too. Such a list would function as a demonstration of the ecumenical unity of several groups in early Christianity. The listed groups and individuals are those who must have agreed to call their Easter experience by terms (gospel), images (Jesus' death as sacrifice), and categories (the apocalyptic resurrection) which were used in the Formula of Faith.[3]

However, Paul used the list with a second intention, too. The fact that he stressed that he was the last one of the apostles means that there are no apostles after him. It follows that those who preach and teach the wisdom of the risen Lord (cf. 1 Cor 1:22) and are not in accordance with the formula are not authentic apostles. The authentic apostles are those listed above, Paul being the last witness of Jesus' appearances. It is obvious that those who denied the hope of resurrection do not belong to the authoritative group, nor do any who were presenting any other new teachings allegedly derived from their direct contact with the risen Lord.

1.2.10 Other Christologies

At this point, we encounter a serious problem of Early Christian Christologies. In 1 Cor 15, Paul quotes the Formula of Faith in order to refute a false teaching which, as we have mentioned, in

However, this suggestion that Jesus developed, in fact, a modern, liberal religion, which subsequently was confirmed by framing his activity with a Redeemer Myth, was radically challenged by Albert Schweitzer (1875–1965) in his "The Mystery of the Kingdom of God" (1901) and his voluminous book *The Quest of the Historical Jesus*.[6] Schweitzer went through the Jewish apocalyptic writings that were accessible in his time and derived Jesus' proclamation of the kingdom from the apocalyptic expectation of a cataclysm at the end of this age and before the beginning of the age to come. This is, according to him, the decisive feature of Jesus' expectation. His radical ethic of love is radical because it was designed for the supposed short period before the cosmic catastrophe through which the new world will arise. Jesus considered himself to be the eschatological prophet of the reign of God, but since his proclamation did not find the expected answer in Israel, he decided to provoke its coming by his own suffering. He was the Messiah without his messianic empire—the Messiah without the messianic age. Nevertheless, his moral effort has been inspiring till the present time.

Of course, this can be called Christology only in a very metaphorical sense. Schweitzer's life work in Lambarene on behalf of poor people is a convincing demonstration of how even the radically reduced living heritage of Jesus may be effective.

For a long time Schweitzer led Jesus research, at least in German-speaking countries. It was only Adolf von Harnack (1851–1930) who did not lose his confidence in the basic reliability of the synoptic tradition, especially of its image of God as the father of all humans and of humankind as his family. In the British scene, a similar interpretation was presented by A. C. Headlam (1862–1947) in his book, *The Life and Teaching of Jesus the Christ* (1923).

1.3.3 From Dodd and Bultmann to the New Quest

The main weakness of Schweitzer's method was his uncritical interpretation of the Matthean and Markan narrative frame as a source reflecting historical reality. Further investigation has shown that the frame of the narrative is secondary, derived according to the Two Sources Theory from the Gospel of Mark.

It was Charles H. Dodd (1884–1973) who, in the English-speaking areas, proposed an alternative interpretation. According to Dodd, a close link between the kingdom and Jesus is typical of the synoptic tradition. In his ministry, the kingdom of God was "realized." So Jesus, as the teller of the parables of the kingdom, is in his present activity identical with agents of the first part of several parables, e.g., with the sower from the well-known parable (Mark 4:1–9), so that he directly introduced the kingdom.[7]

In spite of all drawbacks of his method (especially underestimating the influence of apocalypticism), Dodd did not neglect the historical findings and enabled the reader to experience the **eschaton** as transcendence confronting one with the present dimension of the kingdom in Jesus' proclamation.

Meanwhile, German research became oriented toward an analytical investigation of the synoptic tradition and its function in Christian proclamation and liturgy in the first generations. It was Martin Dibelius and Rudolf Bultmann (1884–1976) who started the so-called school of form criticism. From the literary shape of individual smaller units of the synoptic tradition, they attempted to deduce the function of the units in the life of early Christian groups in Palestine and their development in the Greek-speaking Hellenistic Christian communities through subsequent generations.

Bultmann shared the following premises with the previous liberal period of Jesus research. The Christ Myth depends on a world view which was different from our image of the world, so that, in the present proclamation, it could not function as it did at the beginning. Yet, he started a monumental attempt at a new interpretation of the Easter **kerygma** for his contemporaries.[8] He interpreted the "mythical" proclamation in terms of Heidegger's philosophy of existence and of Dilthey's psychological **hermeneutics**: It is the faith of believers answering the proclamation of the crucified Jesus as Savior that opens the way toward the real Easter. In this respect, the understanding precedes the interpretation; interpretation is an additional process helping the believer to understand himself and to communicate his/her faith. Easter is recognizable as an individual new understanding of existence in its openness toward the future.

Bultmann's image of Jesus was limited to his self-understanding and to the mere *that* of his existence in history.

Bultmann's students decided to link the new and "open" Christian self-understanding with the self-understanding of Jesus. For Ernst Fuchs (1903–1983), Jesus was the founder of faith as personal relation to God; he was the pioneer of faith (cf. Heb 12:2). This is the decisive motif that inspired James M. Robinson's *The New Quest for Historical Jesus* (1959). He was aware of the fact that, methodically, it is impossible to reconstruct a life of Jesus; but, according to him, there is a direct way from the unique self-understanding of Jesus to explain the rise of alternative Christologies of Early Christianity. Robinson, together with Helmut Koester, characterized several christological streams that are recognizable in the early Christian literature:[9] an apocalyptic Christology of the Son of Man (see §3.1.2); the Christology of (Jesus as) a Divine Man, which is typical of the synoptic miracle stories; the Christology of Jesus as the always valid wisdom (Gr. *sofia*; see §3.1.3) as it is in the source of Sayings (Q) or in the *Gospel of Thomas;* and, of course, the Christologies that are included in the Formula of Faith (see §1.2).

The sociohistorical contribution of Gerd Theissen[10] supported the investigation of Jesus' activity as the starting point of any reflection on his significance. He supposed that Christianity originated in various groups of Jesus' adherents in Galilee and neighboring territories. This can be (very roughly) considered to be a sociological counterpart of the alternative Christologies of the New Quest.

The New Quest, especially its hypothesis about various alternative Christologies, was attacked since it is very difficult to prove that the various Christologies represent different groups of the Christian movement. We do have evidence of various Christian groups—James's group in Jerusalem, a Hellenistic party in Jerusalem (Stephen), Apollos in Alexandria, Paul and at least three groups of his successors, a Markan group, a Lukan congregation, a Matthean group, a Johannine school, etc.—but none of them may be explicitly identified with any of the Christologies mentioned above. This is not to say that there were no such Christologies; just that, in Early Christianity, alternative Christologies only for a very short time resisted the tendency toward integration with the resurrection/exaltation Christology.[11]

1.3.4 The Literary Approach

In 1964, Amos N. Wilder published his book *Early Christian Rhetoric,* and the literary approach to New Testament studies started to gain ground. Concurrently, the biblical text became interesting for many scholars who specialized in the theory of literature.

It was especially the discovery of some not yet completely understood functions of language that inspired that change in orientation. The new language theory, introduced by the French scholar Ferdinand de Saussure, discovered the active role of language in organizing the human world (1916). Any sentence (i.e., the basic unit of a language) includes a selection (not everything is worth mentioning) and evaluation of issues it is dealing with. Putting these into a structure established by grammar creates a "text world." The text world is by no means an illusion, since as speaking and reading beings we live in it, and our experience of social relations (I—you—he/she), as well as of time (present—past—future), is organized by language.

In terms of methodology, this means that the starting point of every christological discussion has to be, not the reconstructed earliest stratum of the tradition, but the text units of the New Testament. For example, the primary function of narratives about Jesus' miracles, such as Mark 4:35–41 (Calming the Storm), has to be derived from its context (in this case it is confirming the authority of the parable-tellers) and from the structure of the story itself (in this case to demonstrate that to believe Jesus, who is representing God, the Creator, and not only to rely on miracles, is the appropriate attitude in a crisis). The reconstruction of the pre-history of a text is the second step, and only the fact that the text may point behind itself and reveal its earlier function entitles us to do it. Any integrated hermeneutics has to start with texts.

As with every new insight, the importance of this observation was initially overestimated and one-sidedly interpreted. However, the best representatives of this school are well aware of its limitations and have already opened discussion of the principal problem of interpretation: Is it possible to develop a text theory in such a way that it becomes an integrated hermeneutics, or will it always be necessary to combine various approaches and coordinate them according to a philosophical or theological meta-theory? For example, if we look at the figure below, representing the structure of a text and its relation to the narrated (discussed) world as well as to the world of the interpreter, as it has been offered by V. K. Robbins,[12] we realize that the rhetorical approach has already developed into a complex system of interpretation. To "read" such a figure is as instructive as reading an essay. However, such a figure has to be commented on. And there are some functions which could only be expressed by a multidimensional figure. In discussing Christology, it is, e.g., extremely important to express the relation of the real author to the information the text is handing over—in this case as a testimony. Such an extreme case can demonstrate that the comment on the rhetorical structure always transcends the literary approach itself. It reflects its conditions, introduces intention and subjectivity (especially when speaking on testimony), and invites the scholar as well as the reader of such an investigation to his or her own decision.

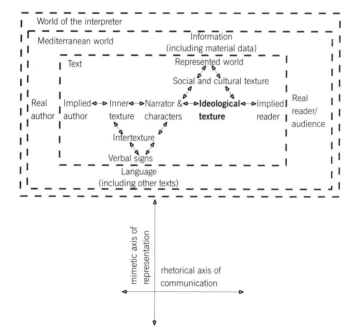

The linguistic approach brought new insights to many individual problems, especially regarding the function of individual text categories. For example, Vernon K. Robbins developed a complex socio-rhetorical model of textual communication.[13] As for the Jesus tradition, the scholars of this school rediscovered the rhetorical channels through which the stories about Jesus were handed down. The role of their spontaneous liturgical shaping was not so great as the German school of form criticism had supposed, and their transmission by means of semiprofessional rhetorical formation has obviously been the decisive influence.

This does not mean that the Christian community was passive in christological discussion, yet it was active rather as a more or less active receptor, not so much as an author or editor: e.g., Christian communities preferred some traditions which were not supported by several prominent leaders, such as Paul (especially the tradition of miracles of Jesus; see 1 Cor 1:22), so that eventually the Gospel writers forged them into a new christological frame.

In general terms, the findings of the literary approach strengthened confidence in the reliability of Jesus tradition and indirectly initiated a series of christological projects based on the teaching of earthly Jesus and his activity, often called the "Third Quest for Historical Jesus." E. P. Sanders, for example, interpreted Jesus as a Jewish reformer promoting the religious concept of "covenantal nomism" against temple-centered piety.[14]

Another group of scholars from the American Jesus Seminar, who may be called neoliberals, tried to interpret Jesus as a wise man—a Jewish philosopher of a certain school—on the model of ancient Cynic philosophers.

1.4 Methodology

1.4.1 From the Biblical Text to Jesus of Nazareth

As we have just demonstrated, the text is the starting point for all our investigation. Yet, since the oldest texts about Jesus (most of them are included in the New Testament) (a) proclaim him to be a representative of God himself and (b) still identify

him with Jesus of Nazareth, we have to gather as much historical evidence about his life and his teaching as possible. Even in
New Testament times, Christians realized that the statements of
their faith and their proclamation could and should be tested as
to whether they are in accordance with the earthly Jesus, or at
least that they do not oppose him: "This is how you can recognize the Spirit of God; every spirit which confesses that Jesus
Christ has come in the flesh is from God." (1 John 4:2; cf.
2 John 7). The earthly Jesus has been called the feedback of
Christian faith. This is the reason why we start our study of New
Testament Christology with an investigation of Jesus' life
and teaching.

To get a reliable image of Jesus means to start with information which is attested by at least two independent witnesses.
This is quite difficult since, according to this premise, we may
know for certain only the few features of his life which are
shared by the Pauline epistles and the synoptic tradition: He
was a Jew (Gal 4:4); he had brothers (1 Cor 9:5), one of them
being James (Gal 1:19; cf. 1 Cor 15:7); he gathered disciples,
one of them being Cephas, called also Peter (Gal 2:1–14; 1 Cor
9:5, cf. 1 Cor 15:5a); and another was John (Gal 2:9).

As to the information included in the Gospels, we may start
only with sayings that are attested in the Gospel according to
Mark as well as in the source of Jesus' sayings (Q) on which
Luke and Matthew are dependent in the passages that are common to both of them and are not derived from Mark. Such a
double-attested text is, for instance, the saying about faith mov-
ing a mountain (Matt 17:20 [Q]; Mark 11:22–23). However,
this is a meager set of information.

Fortunately, the methodology of historical research allows
us to replace the second independent witness with a conclusion
that the author of a bit of information had nothing to gain by
creating it. For example, the fact that Jesus was baptized by
John the Baptist (Mark 1:9–11) is obviously an authentic one,
since Christians tended to stress the dominance of Jesus over
John the Baptist. It is unlikely that such an event, which tends to
enhance the role of John the Baptist, would be fabricated.

The generalized rule developed for this methodology is
called the criterion of dissimilarity. By it, we accept as authentic

The Good Shepherd was not a specifically Christian image, but it appealed to many Christians because of their understanding of Christ as their shepherd. It was very common among Early Christian symbols and can be found on sarcophagi, paintings, murals, etc.

Above is a drawing of part of an ancient Christian Roman sarcophagus with the image of the Good Shepherd in the center.

To the left is a marble statue of the Good Shepherd from Rome of the late third century CE.

Above, a mosaic of Christ the Good Shepherd on the entrace wall of the Mausoleum of Galla Placidia in Ravenna, Italy (ca. 450 CE).

Below, a mosaic in the Church of Saint Apollinare, also in Ravenna. Note the beardless Jesus in both images.

Two images from the ancient catacombs. Above, a mosaic of a bearded Jesus. Below, a reconstruction of a wall drawing from the catacombs of San Callisto (mid-third century CE).

Above, another mosaic from Ravenna, this one depicting Christ before Pilate. Below is the marble sarcophagus of Junius Bassus (ca. 359 CE). Bassus was a prefect of the city of Rome, who converted to Christianity on his deathbed. He was buried in St. Peter's next to the apostle's tomb. His sarcophagus has several biblical scenes, each put in its own frame. The frame at the top right shows Jesus before Pilate.

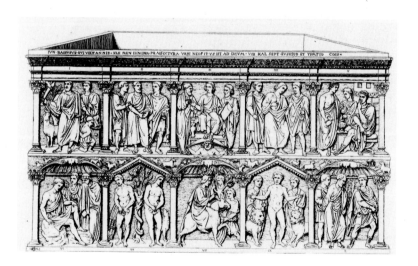

Above is a drawing of a fifth-century Roman ivory panel which depicts the crucifixion and shows Judas having hanged himself.

To the left is a fourth-century drawing of the Samaritan woman at the well, with Jesus watching her draw water.

Above, the arrest of Christ, a sixth-century mosaic at Saint Apollinare in Ravenna.

Below, a drawing of the center of a dome mosaic over the Orthodox Baptistry at Ravenna, depicting the baptism of Jesus (ca. 458 CE).

This is a sixth-century Coptic ivory carving which depicts the miracle of converting water to wine at Cana. In this image, a bearded Jesus supervises the pouring of the water. Coptic art comes from the upper Nile Valley of Egypt.

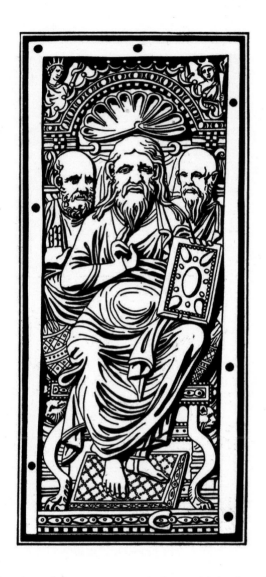

This is a drawing of the center panel of a multiple diptych of ivory, which probably originated in Alexandria, Egypt, in the sixth century. It shows an enthroned Christ with Peter and Paul. Similar work was done at the same time in Antioch and Syria, often showing a beardless Jesus.

Jesus tradition all that cannot be interpreted either as a typical expression of Jewish thinking or of the later Christian community.[15]

Since that which we can establish by this means is still very limited, it is necessary to combine the criterion of dissimilarity with the criterion of coherence. This means that we take the information established according to the criterion of dissimilarity as the starting point and ask about its compatibility with the other pieces of information.

1.4.2 The Problem with Easter

We turn now to the basic problem of New Testament Christology: Why did Jesus become God's representative and the bearer of decisive hope in all Christian texts? How are we to deal with this "divine" dimension of his phenomenon?

Ecclesiastical Christology is based only on the testimony of the first Christian generation. Nevertheless, even such a testimony can be at least indirectly proved. We may ask whether it is congruent; whether the witnesses are able to reflect their testimony and express it in an alternative way; whether they are able to communicate with people of other opinions; whether, when assuming the authenticity of their witness, we may better understand history; whether it is spontaneous; and whether it is linked with any pressure on the addressees. After the witness stands up to such an examination, it has to be taken seriously. We can never say that the authenticity of such an engaged witness is absolutely proved, but we may say that under such conditions, the witness has to be taken seriously.

The result of all such examination is that the witness has to be taken seriously in the sense that we must engage our own decision-making processes when accepting or rejecting it. This is implicit in every sort of testimony. It does not mean that a discipline dealing with a testimony (as in this case, theology) transcends science. As long as we consider humanities to be a special kind of scientific research, we must not exclude theology from its company. Law and history, as important as they are, are also based on testimony. In theology, the specific features of this approach are only more visible, since the impact of the testimony is deeper. They call everybody into the position of a judge, they call people to decision, and it is impossible to remain neutral and yet be interested in these matters. The only attitude which may be called "objective" is one which openly acknowledges its own decisions—which takes into account the way the scholar answered the challenge of the texts. This is the irreversible common denominator of post-positivistic research and the hermeneutics of testimony, as it was developed by Jean Nabert and Paul Ricoeur. Admittedly, there are scholars who try to restore positivistic premises;[16] but, on the whole, the issue is closed.

Jesus

A s we have mentioned, it is appropriate to start our study with an investigation of the Jesus tradition, even though the synoptic Gospels are considerably later than the letters of Paul.

2.1 Jesus' Proclamation

We have already mentioned some data from Jesus' life which is attested both by the Gospels and by Paul. Since his life and his behavior were undoubtedly linked closely to his proclamation and teaching, we open our investigation by discussing his central idea: the kingdom of God. In Paul, the term "kingdom of God" does not play any decisive role. Yet, he tries to interpret its meaning in a new way (Rom 14:17).[1] This fact speaks for the authenticity of the kingdom of God in Jesus' teaching.

2.1.1 Jesus' Rhetoric
The proclamation and teaching on the kingdom of God has been preserved in several rhetorical (literary) forms: parable, beatitude, prayer, prophetic saying, and wisdom. It was only Matthew who, in a good Jewish way, spoke about the kingdom of Heaven.

There are several parallels to the idea of kingdom of God in the Old Testament and in more or less contemporary Jewish texts.[2] Perhaps the closest parallel is the Kaddish prayer ("May he [God] establish his kingdom in our lifetime . . ."). However, the consistent use of the phrase "kingdom of God" is typical only of the synoptic tradition.

In terms of modern linguistics, the phrase "kingdom of God" is a metaphor—a preliminary signal of a reality which does not yet belong to the daily experience and which has to be illuminated through other metaphors and tested by examining its practical consequences.[3] This is what Jesus did when saying: "The kingdom of God is as if someone would . . ." (Mark 4:26) or "With what can we compare the kingdom of God . . . ?" (4:30) or proclaiming the eucharistic table fellowship to be the link connecting this age with the kingdom of God (Mark 14:25; Luke 22:15–18). The frequent use of parables was obviously typical of Jesus' language.

This reveals that Jesus did not want to take up any of the given images of the kingdom without transformation.

A trace of Jesus' proclamation of the kingdom of God may be the expression "kingless (race)." Earlier it was known from extra-canonical writings, but the Nag Hammadi texts confirm that it was a phrase with important connotations.[4] Since kingdom is not an idea typical of Gnostic systems, this may have been derived from Jesus' proclamation of kingdom or preserved from non-Christian (Jewish?) sources.[5] In Matt 19:28, we read about the disciples of Jesus as those who will share the royal throne with the Son of Man (cf. Rev 3:21). So the Christian Gnostics considered themselves to be a kingless or undominated race of kings themselves.[6]

Since the Gnostic texts are all later than the Gospels, this could be only a secondary development. Yet, in 1 Cor 4:8, Paul with irony criticizes an enthusiastic group of Corinthian Christians saying: "without us you became kings." From the context, we may deduce that these people already enjoyed the fulfillment of Jesus' Beatitudes that we know from the Sermon on the Mount.[7] This is a kind of spiritual interpretation of Jesus' social dimension of the kingdom, as it is attested in several sayings in the *Gospel of Thomas*. Since the Corinthian correspondence originates from the 50s, the tendencies similar to that evidenced by the phrase "kingless race" are rooted in the Christian tradition prior to the Gospels. They are a valuable evidence of an alternative interpretation of the kingdom of God tradition. This does not mean that such an interpretation originates in Jesus' preaching itself. It only means that Jesus' proclamation of the

kingdom has been effective and attractive for new interpretations in various Christian groups for several generations.

Several times, the synoptic tradition speaks of the kingdom
of God that has come near (Mark 1:15; Matt 4:17; 10:7; Luke
10:9, 11). These are obviously translations of a typical phrase of
Jesus stressing the imminent influence of the kingdom of God.

√ ## 2.1.2 The Kingdom of God in Jesus' Proclamation

The Jewish expectation of God's Reign was closely linked with
the idea of Jewish domination over pagan nations (Mic 5:6–8;
Dan 2:44). Qumran texts confirm the popularity of this expectation in the Essene community.[8] An Israel-centered kingdom is
predicted in Isa 24:23; 33:17–24; and *Jubilees* 1:28.

Isaiah 61 also announces the Reign of God over the nations
as the good news, and Isa 61:1–2a is several times quoted or
alluded to in the Jesus tradition (Luke 7:22c [Q]; Luke 4:18–19;
cf. Acts 10:38). This all may be an ecclesiastical attempt to
legitimate the post-Easter gospel through the authority of the
Scripture. However, Isa 61:1–2a also influenced the introduc-
tory Beatitudes from the Sermon on the Plain/Mount (Luke
6:20–21) without being quoted. This means that Isa 61:1–2a
was not added later as additional support, but that it was a part
of the pre-Easter tradition from the beginning. Consequently,
we have to suppose at least some prophetic messianity in Jesus'
self-understanding. This means that even the term for bringing
good news (Heb. *biśśar*, Gr. *euaggelizein*) and for the good news
itself (see §1.2.2) could possibly be derived from his preaching
and teaching.

Some of Jesus' acts and decisions may be understood in
light of these traditions. When, from the obviously larger group
of his disciples, he appointed the Twelve (Mark 3:14), it obviously was a symbolic interpretation of his activity as fulfillment
of a similar expectation of the kingdom among the twelve tribes
of Israel. The same was indicated by the **pericope** of the Syro-
phenician Woman's Faith (Mark 7:24–30), where Jesus proclaimed his activity to be concentrated on Israel, as well as by his
instruction given to his disciples proclaiming the kingdom of
God: "Go nowhere among the Gentiles . . . but go rather to the
lost sheep of Israel" (Matt 10:5–6; 15:24). These are obviously
authentic features of his activity, since the post-Easter

Christianity tried to relativize them, and Luke did not accept them into his Gospel.

This does not mean that Jesus did not include the nations into his expectation of the kingdom, it rather means that, according to him, the universal and ecumenic kingdom of God was also Israel-centered and that he expected the pilgrimage of nations to Jerusalem (Isa 11:10; 19:19–25; 60; 66:19–20; Mic 4:1–8; Zech 8:20–23). He intended to prepare Israel to accept them, to make it the "priestly kingdom and a holy nation" (Exod 19:6).

Thus, it must have been quite a surprise to have heard the statement of Jesus in Q about the people from east and west who will participate in the kingdom of God together with Abraham, whereas some Jews may be thrown out (Q [Luke] 13:28–29). His Israel-centered expectation is not necessarily an Israel-dominated kingdom, and it is even possible that some prominent Jews will be excluded. The pre-Easter origin of this sentence is supported by the fact that it supposes the Israel-centered ecumenicity of the kingdom.

The parable of the Great Dinner (Luke 14:15–24) should be understood in terms of this prophetic warning. It certainly was adapted by the Gospel writers to fit the ecclesiastical model of an extensive mission. It is also obvious that it did not speak about the universality of the kingdom, but it makes us aware of the fact that Jesus' proclamation announced a reversal of fates and that his relation to the sinners was not limited by the borders established by the religious orthodoxy of his time. The problem was not the particularity or universality (ecumenicity) of the kingdom, it was rather the fact that the sinners, the unworthy, were also invited to participate. The popularity of this parable in various Christian groups is confirmed by its parallel in the *Gospel of Thomas* (Log. 64).

Some Qumran texts may help us to understand the specific prophetic function of this parable and similar happenings initiated by Jesus. In 1QM 7.4–6, or 11Q19 (= *Temple Scroll*) 45.12–14, we read that the lame, blind, and crippled are not allowed to enter the community either in war or in worship. Jesus' table fellowship with sinners and his exhortation to invite the poor, lame, crippled, and blind for table fellowship in Luke

14:13 or his parallel saying in the parable on the Great Banquet
(Luke 14:21) could be understood as an expression of a con-
scious distance from the Qumran concept of purity and salvation.[9]

2.1.3 Love of Enemies

At first glance, the commandment of love including also the
enemies (Q [Luke] 6:27; *Didache* 1.3; cf. Rom 12:14; 1 Cor
4:12) appears to be a radical, morally more demanding version
of the Old Testament love commandment (Deut 6:5 and Lev
19:18; see Mark 12:29–31; cf. Rom 13:9; Gal 5:14; James
2:8). In fact, it is rooted deeper, i.e., in the character of the kingdom as a universal promise. "To love" does not mean that the
disciples of Jesus should try to fall into sentimental love with
their adversaries, neither that in love with them they would
accept their perverted demands. The Jesus tradition as a whole
reveals that his love included in some cases a warning, in others
a demand to follow him. From the direct context of the love
command in both Luke and Matthew, we may deduce that this
love reflects the mercy of God which was included in his invita-
tion to the kingdom. To love somebody means to bless him or
her (Luke 6:28), i.e., to wish that person everything good from
God. The phrase "to pray for" in verse 28 has the same meaning. "Everything good" in the context of Jesus' proclamation is
God's kingdom. That "to love" means to wish somebody the
kingdom can be deduced also from the opposite point of view,
which is cursing (v. 28a).

What we have demonstrated by now, and what is obviously
included in the oldest stratum of Jesus tradition, is that there
was a close link between the kingdom of God as a promised
future—as a given hope—and the moral radicalism of Jesus. In
principle, the radicality was not motivated by the near coming
of the kingdom, as Schweitzer supposed (see §1.3.2), but by its
overwhelming positive value.

In Matthew, the phrase "love your enemies" is introduced
by quoting an opposite demand: "You have heard that it was
said, 'You shall love your neighbor (see Lev 19:18) and hate
your enemy.' But I say to you, Love your enemies . . ." (Matt
5:43–44a). However, except for some sentences about the
prosecution of specific adversaries of Israel (Deut 25:19, etc.),

we do not find any commandment of hatred against enemies in all the Old Testament; so Matt 5:43 evokes a false anti-Jewish sentiment. The absolute love command can be found in at least one stream of Jewish wisdom, where it is represented by Jesus the Son of Sirach from the second century BCE: "He that takes vengeance will suffer vengeance from the Lord . . . set enmity aside . . ." (Sir 28:1, 6). To "do good to your friends and to do harm to your enemies" was rather a Greek maxim.[10]

The only Jewish parallels are to be found in the *Manual of Discipline* of the Essene sect from Qumran. They were forbidden to do any harm to their adversaries (1QS 10.17–18) before the eschatological struggle led by legions of angels should begin.[11] Nevertheless, they were admonished to hate them.[12] The reason was obvious: an awareness of the difference between good and bad should be preserved. As we shall see (§2.2), at the beginning of his activity, Jesus was influenced by John the Baptist, whose apocalyptic ideas were similar to those of the Qumran group. So, "Love your enemies" may have been consciously formulated as an alternative to the principle of moral behavior represented in the manual of Qumran.[13] Matthew revealed the hidden code that was necessary for understanding Jesus' saying about absolute love in the second or third Christian generation. Jesus' refusal of possible help from his father, who could send him twelve legions of angels, which is interwoven into the Matthean passion story in Matt 26:53, confirms that some Qumranic ideas represented in the *War Scroll*[14] were familiar to the Gospel writer or to his immediate sources.

2.1.4 The Kingdom of God and the Present: Jesus as a Messianic Prophet or as a Teacher of Wisdom?

The age to come is not yet present. It is different from the present age (cf. Mark 10:30), whereas the kingdom of God is so near (see §2.1.1) that it immediately affects our present. These are two alternative images that can be combined, but they cannot be fully harmonized.

According to the Gospels, Jesus proclaimed the near kingdom (e.g., in Mark 1:15; see §2.1.2), yet according to the Q source, he can say also that the kingdom of God "has come upon you" (Luke 11:20). And, according to Luke (17:21), he dared to say that the kingdom of God "is in the midst of you."

Obviously, all these phrases translate various expressions of the same phenomenon, only the stress has shifted. The Lukan phrase may relate to Jesus who incorporates the kingdom in the present, but even if it is a Lukan sentence, it (maybe one-sidedly) reflects the intention of the older tradition. This means that the kingdom of God, undoubtedly expected as a reality drawing near in the temporal sense, has also another dimension of its imminence, that its impact upon the present belongs to its substance. The *Gospel of Thomas* even supposes the presence of the kingdom in (the souls of) the believers.[15]

These observations concerning specific features of the kingdom of God proclamation in early Jesus traditions are very important since they call into question the apocalyptic model of Jesus' message that has become common in post-Schweitzer research (especially since they reveal an intentional selection and transformation—innovation—of ideas, motifs, and images of his time in Jesus' proclamation and teaching). Once we recognize how he transformed the idea of the kingdom of God, we understand better that he was able to argue by means of a theology of creation (Matt 5:45) and that, beside the kingdom imagery, he was also able to speak about the Son of Man without mixing these two sets of images together. Some scholars in the 1950s and 1960s concluded that only one of these images (kingdom and Son of Man) can be authentic. Yet, it is more probable that Jesus, as far as we can judge from the earliest traditions, availed himself with more than one set of images and used them alternatively. In other words, one possible interpretation of the critical findings concerning the earliest Jesus traditions is to respect their variety and to admit that he used them according to a **didactic** strategy that was not dependent upon only one particular tradition.

2.1.4.1 The Hypothesis of a Non-Eschatological Jesus

These facts caused several scholars to declare that the apocalyptic features are a secondary post-Easter layer of Jesus tradition.[16] Their thesis is a sound reaction against apocalyptic interpretations that did not recognize the specific features of Jesus' kingdom of God proclamation. However, they suppose that, together with the apocalyptic impact, all the elements which could have been considered the starting point of Jesus'

post-Easter christological and soteriological (salvific) significance are secondary in the synoptic tradition. In our opinion,
there are several obstacles that prevent us from accepting a
non-eschatological image of Jesus as a Jewish teacher of wisdom, similar to a Cynic philosopher.

One necessary condition for a non-eschatological Jesus was
a stratification of Q that would prove that all the apocalyptic
sayings belong in a secondary layer.[17] However, it is very difficult to declare, for example, that the saying ". . . whoever
acknowledges me before men, the Son of Man will also
acknowledge him before the angels of God" (Luke 12:8; cf. v. 9
[Q]), which is attested also by Mark (8:38), is secondary, while
the counterpart, "All things have been committed to me by my
Father . . ." (Luke 10:22; cf. v.21) belongs to the earliest layer.
The first saying, which did not yet identify Jesus with the Son of
Man and has been corrected in Matthew to read ". . . I will also
acknowledge him" (Matt 10:32), is definitely an old saying,
since already in Paul's time, the apocalyptic messianic title Son
of Man was losing its significance. Even if we cannot exclude
the possibility that there was a short post-Easter period in which
the activity of Jesus was immediately linked with the expected
Son of Man, so that "Son of Man" could be a secondary inser-
tion, the clause (the so-called Clause of the Sacred Law) would
express the eschatological key position of Jesus anyway. On the
other hand, the statement of Jesus in Luke 10:22 (Q) was
already shaped in terms of religious language of self-revelation,
which is attested in such writings as the Gospel of John or the
Gnostic tractate on the *Trimorphic Protennoia*[18] from about
200 CE.

Likewise, it is very difficult to remove from the oldest stratum the eschatological saying of Jesus about the Son of Man
coming like a thief (Luke 12:39–40 [Q]), which is frequently
attested in various strata of early Christian tradition (1 Thess
5:2; 2 Pet 3:10; Rev 3:3 and 16:15 as words of Jesus), and even
the *Gospel of Thomas* (log. 21) had to accept it. The same may
be said about the Lord's Prayer ("Thy kingdom come!"), which
mostly is considered to be a part of Q.[19]

It is difficult to divorce the New Testament Son of Man
sayings from the apocalyptic Son of Man tradition by declaring

that in many instances this may be only a designation of a human being. The most solid study of this kind is by D. Hare (1990), but in view of Mark 8:38 and other evidence, it is clear that a part of the Son of Man sayings represents an apocalyptic dimension which cannot be removed from the earliest Jesus tradition.

Eschatological and soteriological features are also inseparably interwoven in the passion story; so that to maintain the image of Jesus as a teacher of wisdom means to prove that the passion story is secondary—that it was composed by Mark and/or that a part of it (the story of crucifixion) originates from the *Gospel of Peter*. We shall discuss this problem in the last part of this book.

2.1.4.2 Conclusions
The present impact of the kingdom is obviously only one dimension of its complex reality; it may be understood as an anticipation of its full presence. Only in a few instances is faith expressly related to the kingdom of God (Mark 1:14–15). Nevertheless, throughout the Jesus tradition, focus on the kingdom is directed toward faith and the future: ". . . whatever you ask in prayer, believe that you have received it, and it will be yours" (Mark 11:24); or "Amen, I tell you, if you have faith as a mustard seed, you will say to this mountain 'Move from here to there' and it will move and nothing will be impossible to you" (Matt 17:20). Even in the stories where the believer's orientation toward the future has reached its aim in the period which is present from the teller's point of view, it is clear that the fulfilled faith opens a new prospect and a new expectation—from discipleship to the absolute future ("all is possible to him who believes"—Mark 9:23). The other side of faith is obviously the "do not worry" or "do not be anxious" (Luke 12:22–34), the "cares of this life" being its opposite (Luke 21:34; cf. Phil 4:6). So faith is the opposite of despair, doubt, anxiety, isolation, and of a fatal view of the world.

Comparing two well-known sayings about the mustard seed, we may indirectly describe the relationship between the present and the future dimension of the kingdom: one is the just quoted saying about the faith as mustard seed; the other is the parable of the Mustard Seed (Mark 4:30–32), according to which, in the present, the kingdom of God is like a mustard seed. Well aware of the fact that according to all traditions Jesus used various systems of images (the coming kingdom, God as Creator, faith, Son of Man) which cannot be harmonized into an ideology, we still may metaphorically express the two dimensions of the kingdom of God in his teaching (the present one and the future one) by saying that *faith is the present shape of the kingdom*. Its fulfillment is a future, "eschatological" reality (in the sense of the "coming" future which cannot be grasped by **prognostics**), which has a social dimension (see the tree as an image of the kingdom of Israel in Ezek 17:22–24) and represents the absolute future as a home ("the birds of heavens have nests in its shade"—nest is a symbol of home in all cultures).

This two-pole image of the kingdom of God in Jesus' teaching better corresponds to the texts than the image of the kingdom of God as an alternative model of society in the **pedagogical** strategy of a wisdom teacher.[20] No doubt, Jesus was a teacher, and many contemporaries used to address him Rabbi, "teacher" (*didaskalos*; John 1:38). Indeed, the synoptic tradition reveals that the Pharisees—adherents of the most influential Jewish reform movement—were his closest discussion partners. Nevertheless, his self-understanding was not limited by his role as a teacher in the rabbinic sense (Matt 23:7–8). Rather, he was a teaching prophet.

His interpretation of the love commandment, absolute in its validity and yet totally non-moralistic, and his concept of the kingdom as a real future of this world and as an alternative model of relations among humans and between humans and God, as well as his concept of the kingdom with its impact on the present, even if we know it only in an indirect and fragmentary way, all reveal not only a pious personality, but also an original mind—a *genius*.

2.2 Jesus the Prophet

2.2.1 Prophecy in Jesus' Time

In Jesus' time, "prophet" was a term for religious personalities of various kinds. In Israel, prophets were the men/women whom God had given his Spirit so that they were able to proclaim his will. Prophets did not need to quote the Scripture to support their message. In the Hellenistic and Roman period, there were several influential Jewish groups, such as the Pharisees, which were convinced that the prophetic Spirit has died out in Israel (Ps 74:9). Later, they maintained that it had been replaced by its echo—the rabbinic tradition.[21]

2.2.1.1 The Teacher of Righteousness

The Qumran texts have changed our portrait of the prophetic expectations of Jesus' time. Undoubtedly, the Essenes also considered the prophetic period as a phenomenon of the past,[22] but the Teacher of Righteousness, who must have lived in the late Hellenistic time and whom they considered to be their patron, was considered to speak "from the mouth of God,"[23] and like the prophets,[24] he was called the servant of God.[25] The way he rebuked the highest priest in Jerusalem recalls prophetic authority.[26] He described himself allegorically as an eternal fountain and as the holder of eternal mysteries.[27]

Originally, the Teacher of Righteousness (or the True Teacher) was a real person, a priest from the Zadokite family.[28] As a priest, he also was a teacher.[29] The scholarly community learned about his role in eschatological expectations several decades before the Qumran texts were published from the so-called Zadokite Fragment (*Damascus Document*)—a tractate which was discovered in the Old Cairo Synagogue in 1896. However, the Qumran texts help us to characterize him in a more competent way. In the Qumran commentary on the book of Habakkuk,[30] it is supposed that the Scriptures relate to him. He was *the* prophet (cf. Deut 18:18; Mal 3:23), who was initiated in all the mysteries of God.[31] To be loyal to him is the condition of salvation.[32] After his death, he was probably expected to reappear.[33] Also, it is apparent that he was sentenced to death or murdered by his adversaries.[34] Because of these analogies, several scholars have thought him to be identical with James the Righteous,[35] John the Baptist,[36] or even with Jesus himself.[37] These are very improbable hypotheses, since: (a) they lack any explicit identification of the teacher's adversaries; and (b) all accessible indirect evidence for dating his life indicates that he lived between the mid-second century and the mid-first century

BCE, his opponent thus being either the high priest Alkimos (162–160 BCE), Simon the Maccabee, or some ruler of the Hyrcan dynasty.

2.2.1.2 John the Baptist

Another man who claimed prophetic authority was John the Baptist, even if he did not call himself prophet.[38] He considered himself to be the precursor of the age to come, which would be opened by God's judgment (Mark 1:7–8; Luke 3:7–9 [Q]), indeed, he most probably considered himself to be the new Elijah, the precursor of the "more powerful one"—of God himself (Luke 3:16ff. [Q], cf. Mal 3:1ff., 11). John introduced baptism as a unique act: (a) anticipating the judgment and serving as a kind of individual catharsis, as a shocking experience which caused reappraisal of values (mere membership in God's people does not guarantee salvation); and (b) thereby as a promise of surviving God's judgment (Luke 3:6ff. [Q]). This, in fact, meant a reformation of Israel as God's people. John's popularity was enhanced by his martyrdom.

2.2.2 Jesus and John the Baptist

All Christian traditions had to deal with the problem of John's influence on Jesus. In their time, John was the more popular one. Jesus belonged to John's followers, letting himself be baptized by him (Mark 1:9–11). The unrepeatable baptism of John inspired Christians to introduce baptism in Jesus' name in post-Easter time. The fact that Jesus lived in the shadow of John's proclamation and John's fate is evidenced by the rumors that Jesus was John the Baptist raised from the dead (Mark 6:14; 8:28).

The other undeniable fact is that Jesus soon separated from John, gathered his own followers, and had his own students and sympathizers. The pericope on Messengers from John the Baptist (Q [Luke] 7:18–23) reveals an ambivalent relationship between Jesus and John. This itself is a heavy argument in favor of its authentic core.

2.2.3 Prophetic Symbolic Actions

We have already mentioned Jesus' provoking rhetoric. Its counterpart is his provoking activity. This obviously belongs to the category of prophetic symbolic actions, like those performed by the Old Testament prophets.[39] His appointment of a group of twelve as a symbol of the twelve tribes of the renewed God's people is an example of this kind of activity, as was his cleansing of the Temple (Mark 11:15–19; John 2:13–22). Another one of these actions was undoubtedly Jesus' entry into Jerusalem riding a donkey (Mark 11:1–11). The donkey was not a military animal at that time, so that the import of Jesus' entry must have been a kind of performance expressing that the time of fulfillment of God's promises is coming in an unexpected, paradoxical way, as represented in Zech 9:9 by the narrative on the king of peace riding on a donkey.

This does not mean that the story of the entry into Jerusalem was fabricated on the model of Zechariah 9. The fact that Matthew stressed the features of the story which recall Zechariah 9 is an argument against a later attempt to claim fulfillment of Zechariah's prophecy. This could have been deduced from the Matthean version alone. Matthew (I call the Gospel writers by their traditional names) did turn Zechariah's literary parallelism donkey/colt into a narrative, so that, according to Matt 21:7, Jesus came to Jerusalem riding (quite acrobatically) on two animals. But this is just a secondary expansion of the story.

The common denominator of these actions is the anticipation of eschatological fulfillment. They represent the expected kingdom of God as it "has come to us"—the kingdom in its present dimension. If it is so, Jesus' actions must be considered to have been a parallel to his proclamation of the kingdom of God—to his teaching. We have mentioned only three such actions. It is very probable that the miraculous feeding of the multitudes (Mark 6:30–44; 8:1–10; John 6:1–15) was a (repeated) action of similar kind. Yet, the layer of post-Easter eucharistic reminiscences covered its historical core.[40]

In light of these observations, we are able to understand better the stories on table fellowship with Jesus. Like several table fellowships in antiquity, the meals in which Jesus took part also served as occasions to confront opinions and to demonstrate new ideas. The fact that Jesus celebrated meals with the afflicted and with sinners (Mark 2:15–17; Luke 19:5–6; Mark

14:3–9; cf. Luke 7:36–50 and John 12:1–8) makes it quite probable that he used such occasion to initiate symbolic actions demonstrating that the expected kingdom does not exclude outsiders (e.g., the lame, as in Qumran[41]). It follows that the proclaimed kingdom meant a radical change of given values. Thus, such meals were a real anticipation of the coming fulfillment and change (Mark 14:25; Luke 22:16; cf. 1 Cor 11:26b, "until he [Jesus] comes"). His sympathies for the poor (cf. Luke 6:20 [Q]) were not motivated by their moral quality; rather, it was a proclamation of the fact that, in the eschatological kingdom of God, the discrepancy between rich and poor will be abolished.

Furthermore, it is not only social injustice that will be overcome; Jesus' community with sinners also includes what has been called forgiveness. From the texts where the theme of forgiveness explicitly appears, such as Mark 2:5, 7 or Luke 17:4, it can be deduced that the proclamation of forgiveness of people on the margins of society follows from the forgiveness that God is offering humans in his kingdom (Matt 18:23–35).

Here we see a difference between Jesus and John the Baptist. Whereas John supposed that the humble attitude enabling people to accept forgiveness should be reached through proclamation of judgment (Matt 3:1–12),[42] Jesus called people to repentance by proclaiming the kingdom of God as an absolutely positive reality. His call included both sinners and the socially disadvantaged. The popular defamation, hurled at both by their common opponents, confirms this conclusion. John was called demonic because of his ascetic life; Jesus was called glutton and drunkard and a friend of tax collectors and sinners (Luke 7:33–34 [Q]).

2.2.3.1 Jesus' Healings
The synoptic tradition includes several miracle stories that were augmented somewhat by popular tradition. Every spontaneous folk tradition tends to heroize the hero. That is why Paul was quite reserved about the traditions of Jesus' miracles: "For Jews demand signs . . . but we proclaim Jesus, the crucified" (1 Cor 1:22–23). The other and later secondary layer, especially in the narratives on nature miracles, is that of theological symbols. However, there must have been a real core of Jesus' extraordinary deeds, especially the healings, behind the later layers.

Indirect evidence for the activity of itinerant healers is in mysterious document from Qumran, 4Q360 (earlier called 4QTherapeia). It consists of two fragments of a Hebrew manuscript on leather strips dealing with medicine and containing several names, two of them being Peter and Caiphas. The text makes no sense, so that some scholars consider it to be a writing exercise inspired by a medical text. Also, the expression "itinerant" is included. The text can be dated to the first century CE. It cannot be interpreted as a document from the group of Jesus' disciples. However, as it was noted by J. H. Charlesworth,[43] it may indirectly indicate that itinerant healers availed themselves of the knowledge of medical practices, as it is still discernible in Mark 7:31–37 or 8:22–26.

Undoubtedly, Jesus healed many people in a way which must have been extraordinary and which was considered miraculous. There are also some other persons from the first two centuries of our era who had the reputation of miraculous healers, e.g., Chanina ben Dosa and Apollonius of Tyana (both of them about one generation younger then Jesus), as well as others, since Lukianos of Samosata (second century CE) reported on a miraculous healer in his satiric essay *Philopseudes* (Incredulus) as an almost typical figure. The more or less unique features of the synoptic stories about Jesus' healings are: (1) Jesus' comment pointing out the faith of some person involved (not necessarily the sick person, e.g., Q [Luke] 7:9; see §2.1.3.2); and (2) the repeated motif of expelling demons from the sick, which in some cases was linked with a (psychotherapeutic?) dialogue. This was not an unknown motif in contemporary religion.[44] Yet, in Jesus tradition it was a typical feature—an alternative expression of his vision of God's grace and forgiveness, according to which it is possible to save the sinner and abolish evil: "if it is by the finger of God that I cast out demons, then the kingdom of God has come to you" (Q [Luke] 11:20).

2.2.4 Jesus and the Law

Jesus was a Jew, obedient to the divine Law. We have already seen that his interpretation of the Love Commandment may be interpreted as a radical summary of the Mosaic Law, but in fact it reflects the overwhelming positive impact of the kingdom: ". . . the greater righteousness represents simultaneously the product of the presence of the kingdom as well as the basis for entrance into the future consummated kingdom."[45] Jesus did not abolish the Law; yet, through the coming of the kingdom, the Mosaic version and rabbinic interpretation of the Law was relativized.

In most of the Jewish apocalyptic texts of his time, the age to come is characterized, among other things, by a strict observation of God's righteousness,[46] which is obviously the Mosaic Law, though not necessarily the Pharisaic interpretation. This was also an idea of the Qumran community.[47]

As for the Pharisees, they interpreted the Law, as represented in the Torah, by specifying it for the conditions of Hellenistic civilization with its developed trade, urban culture, etc. Their idea was to "make a fence around the Law,"[48] i.e., to formulate detailed instructions in order that the main commandment may not be violated.

Jesus decided on a different interpretation: not by means of a casuistic multiplication, but by a dramatic reduction. His greatest (double) commandment (Mark 12:28–34) is not a mere tentative summary, it must have played a central part in his teaching. We may observe it from its echo in various Early Christian writings (Gal 5:14; Rom 13:9; James 2:8; GosThom 25; Did 1.2).

There are several pieces of tradition which reveal clearly that in the name of the coming kingdom Jesus relativized the Mosaic Law in a very significant way: First, there is a clear expression of a moral interpretation of cultic cleanliness in Mark 7:14–23, which puts in question the pharisaic explanation. This is not unknown in Jewish history (e.g., Isa 1:16), but the radicality with which it is formulated in Jesus tradition introduces an entirely new view of loyalty to the Torah. Similarly, the healing on the Sabbath in Mark 3:1–6 is a story calling into question the pharisaic concept of Law. Only to preserve life was a healing activity allowed on the Sabbath, which was certainly not the case with a withered hand. Most probably, this was also a symbolic action demonstrating a new understanding of righteousness according to the Law.

A still more striking instance is Jesus' saying in Q (Luke) 9:60, "Let the dead bury their own dead." In Matt 8:22 this saying concerned discipleship, in Luke the proclamation of the kingdom of God.[49] The commendability of the request to bury one's dead from the perspective of mainstream Judaism is illustrated by Tob 1:16 – 2:9 (and in Classical Antiquity by Sophocles' *Antigone*). Jesus' saying about the (obviously metaphorically) dead burying the dead makes it difficult to understand Jesus in terms of Jewish groupings of his time.[50]

All of these differences do not mean that Jesus intended to step outside the boundaries of Jewish religion. He most probably intended its radical reformation, and his spiritual struggle was principally an inter-Jewish problem. E. P. Sanders tried to characterize him as a representative of a kind of "covenantal nomism" with a concept of Law different from the Pharisaic one. However, Jesus interpreted the Law (including the least of the commandments) according to its deepest intention, as he did with the Love Commandment. His radicality relativized the traditional concepts of Law—its rabbinic interpretation as well as its Mosaic scriptural layer. Tension between a radical observance and a relativization of the Law was caused by Jesus' attempt to discover the very will of God, so that his observance was not built up on individual commandments. This is why scholars disagree so visibly when discussing Jesus' attitude toward the Law.

The mysterious saying on the validity of Law from Q (Luke) 16:17 (cf. Matt 5:18) may be understood in terms of such a deep righteousness (Matt 5:20)—of a fulfillment in a general sense. So it has been interpreted in Matthew's Gospel: all the Law and the Prophets hang on the Love Commandment (22:40).[51]

The fact that Paul had to struggle for freedom from the individual commandments of the Law as conditions of salvation has been used as an argument against Jesus' radical new interpretation of Law in the sense of fulfilling its deepest intention. If Jesus had relativized the individual commandments by their new interpretation, it would not have been necessary for Paul to support his freedom by teaching justification through faith and by the grace of God. This is the argument of E. P. Sanders.[52] We may object that: (a) every group has a tendency to compromise with its setting, which for early Christians was the synagogue;

(b) Jesus relativized especially the laws of purity, whereas, in the case of Paul, it was first of all circumcision; and (c) there are some hints at his knowledge of Jesus tradition, especially in Rom 14:14, as compared with Mark 7:18–20.

On this subject, we may risk a summary using semi-psychological categories: Jesus' relation to the Law is derived from his relation to God himself. It was the attitude of an immediate filial confidence and obedience which enabled him to relativize the individual commandments of Law. Jesus was *pious* in a deep and authentic way, and therefore he was able to become *liberal*, too. His saying from Matt 11:29–30, "Take my yoke upon you, and learn from me, for I am gentle and humble in heart; and you will find rest for your souls. For my yoke is easy and my burden is light,"[53] is obviously a text reshaped in the post-Easter time by Christian prophets in the "I" style, but may reflect the two sides of Jesus' ethics and can be used as its summary. "Burdens" is used as a metaphor for commandments and prohibitions of Jewish teachers of Law in Matt 23:4.

2.2.5 Jesus and the Temple

Jesus' critical attitude toward some features of a temple-centered piety may be considered a specific feature of his prophetic activity. The most striking expression of this attitude is the incident which is traditionally called the cleansing of the Temple (Mark 11:15–19; John 2:14–16). This was obviously a prophetic symbolic action (see §2.2.3). Were it not a symbolic action (overturning a few tables and holding up some of the passersby), we should expect an immediate intervention of the temple police, and possibly of the Roman army, as was the case in Acts 21:31ff.

Another warning against relying on the Temple was his prophecy regarding the destruction of the Temple in Mark 13:2, which immediately after the fall of Jerusalem was accommodated in order that it may be considered a prediction of the destruction of the Temple in 70 CE. In fact, it was most probably a part of Jesus' proclamation of the kingdom, expressing that in the kingdom there will be a new, eschatological temple, as depicted in Ezek 40:1 – 44:3.

An especially important document which demonstrates that there were such expectations in the time of Jesus is the *Temple Scroll* from Qumran (11Q19), in which we read about an ideal temple (scarcely a model of the Herodian temple, as was maintained by B. Thiering) which in the age to come will be replaced by a new sanctuary "created" by God himself (29:8–10). This is a certain parallel to the expectation of *SibOr* 4:24–39, where the Temple is replaced by a spontaneous piety, or of Rev 21:22ff.: " I saw no temple in the city, for its temple is the Lord God the Almighty and the Lamb."[54] In the speech of Stephen (Acts 7), we find a set of traditions relativizing the Temple (especially Isa 66:1–2). In fact, they are linked with tradition about the dedication of the Temple itself: "But will God dwell on the earth? Even heaven and the highest heaven cannot contain you, much less this house that I have built," says Solomon himself (1 Kings 8:27). According to the small piece of a legend from Matt 17:24–27, Jesus declared his disciples essentially free from the temple tax. The Qumran people were also opposed to the annual half-shekel temple tax (at least as to paying the sum yearly).[55]

2.3 Jesus the Messiah

2.3.1 Messianic Expectations

The prevalent Jewish expectation of a Messiah (or the Anointed One; see §1.2.6) was often[56] associated with restitution of Davidic political rule. The Qumran texts confirmed the existence of another, non-Davidic, priestly (Aaronic) Messiah who seemed to posses a higher authority than the fighting Messiah from the Davidic dynasty.[57] Only a few documents represent the Messiah as an eschatological ruler, as a prince of peace (Ps Sol 17:32; 18:5, 7; 4 Ezra 7:26–35) opening the time of salvation (1QSa 2:12–22) or the general resurrection (*1 Enoch* 52:4; *Syr Bar* 30:1–2). In Dan 7:13, the Son of Man was also considered to be a messianic figure. Compared with the Messiah, the Son of Man was more a transcendent, more supranatural being, proclaiming God's sentence. His function apparently would have been parallel to that of the "Lord" in Ps 110:1–6.

But, in Jesus' time, the evidence of such an expectation is meager.[58]

2.3.1.1 The Suffering Messiah

The tradition of a suffering eschatological key person, such as the servant of Yahweh in Isaiah 53, has been a very appealing basis for interpreting the Christian concept of the crucified Messiah. The prophet proclaimed that his suffering was a substitute one, that he suffered in favor of the "we"—of the sinners (vv. 4ff.). Regardless of the original meaning of Isaiah 53, these verses have been very influential. They can certainly be seen, for instance, to have influenced the image of a messianic figure (The Righteous One) in the Ethiopic *Apocalypse of Enoch*.[59]

Also, the old hymnic praise of a "Pierced One" in Zech 12:10ff. was occasionally understood as a prophecy of a coming Savior (though it originally referred to king Josiah, who was killed in battle; see 2 Kings 23:29). Individual allusions in Christian texts such as John 19:37 or Rev 1:7 confirm that this was an attractive image for Christians. However, the few quotations regarding this which are in the rabbinic traditions cannot have immediately shaped the messianic self-understanding of Jesus. The same applies to the scattered evidence of a "Messiah ben Joseph"—obviously an expression of the old rivalry between two Jewish tribes.

A sensation was evoked by a fragmentary text from Qumran cave four. According to Robert H. Eisenmann,[60] this fragment bore evidence of a crucified Messiah, since frgm. 5, line 4, speaks of a (messianic?) leader and was translated by him as "and they have the leader of the community killed." But this translation proved to be inadequate, so that the recent translators understand the sentence as follows: ". . . and the leader of the community have them killed."[61] It follows that this text says nothing about the death of the Messiah.

In sum: Jesus did not derive his teaching and activity from a commonly known and widely accepted concept of messianity. We have no evidence of Jesus' considering himself to be a "Messiah that is due to die," as it was supposed by Albert Schweitzer.

We are not able to reconstruct his self-understanding, yet we are able to demonstrate his awareness of a specific mission.

2.3.2 The Messianic Good News

We have already mentioned that the dialogue from Q (Luke) 7:18–23 may reflect Jesus' own proclamation and his self-understanding as the proclaimer of God's eschatological fulfillment of his good will.

His understanding of himself as an agent of eschatological change illuminates the strange saying from Luke 12:49: "I came to bring fire to the earth, and how I wish it were already kindled!" The "I came" sayings are secondary summaries of Jesus' activity as whole. But they most probably took up his own expressions. In this case, the mysterious wording as well as its (most probably independent) attestation in the *Gospel of Thomas* 10 and16 and in **Origen**'s (3rd ct.) homily in Jeremiah III.3 hint toward authenticity of the content. No doubt, fire is a symbol of eschatological judgment by conflagration (Ps 66:12; Q [Luke] 3:9; Jude 7), but Luke obviously understood it also as a symbol of the Holy Spirit, as it is attested in Acts 2:3, so that the sentence of fire may be ambiguous, including the motif of judgment and of a catharsis, as well.

Jesus' relation to God as his father, Abba, expressed also in the Lord's Prayer, confirms the positive motivation of his mission.

2.3.3 Jesus and the Son of Man

We are unable to reproduce the voluminous discussion on the Son of Man and the role of this mysterious apocalyptic figure in Jesus' proclamation. The question "Who is this Son of Man" (John 12:34b) is still a current topic of scholarly inquiry.

We have already mentioned some individual observations, especially in the context of Jesus proclaiming future salvation in his message and representing it in his person. The Son of Man sayings come only from the mouth of Jesus and they have an important role in the Gospels. The sayings that assume his apocalyptic function as we know it from *1 Enoch* 37–71 bear the mark of Early Christian expectations of eschatological fulfillment. However, since some of the sayings do not reveal any post-Easter features and are meaningful even if we exclude the term Son of Man, we have to take them very seriously. For example, in Mark 14:62 (where Jesus names the Son of Man as a representative of the heavenly court), the Son of Man stressed only a motif which was by no means influenced by post-Easter Christology and obviously reflects Jesus' own theology. The Son of Man in his coming at the end of this age was considered a guarantee of Jesus' final vindication.[62]

The motif of a court proclaiming God's judgments and confirming the victory of his Law and of his good will as the conclusion of a heavenly (cosmic) conflict and struggle corresponds to the Son of Man concept in Dan 7:13–14, where the Son of Man is still a figure "like a human being" (NRSV), and where his appearance means the end of a series of inhuman governments of the mythic beasts. This motif can be considered a common denominator of several non-Davidic messianic expectations.

Some Qumran texts, especially those written in Aramaic, have contributed to a better understanding of some New Testament ideas of salvation. In 4QAmram b (4Q544, frgm.1) 9ff., we read about Amram's dream in which two beings contend over him. According to fragment 3, they were given authority and, according to fragment 2, one of them was named Malkiresha (Melkiresha), which means "the wicked king" (as opposed to the Melchizedek, "the righteous king"). The other one emerged victorious in the struggle, but his name is missing. One is safe in assuming that it is none other than Melchizedek himself.[63] Since the setting is an apocalyptic one (mediated through a vision), the dispute is obviously a part of the last judgment.[64] This is confirmed by 11QMelchizedek, where Melchizedek is obviously a heavenly figure and his opponent is Belial. As we stated above, Melchizedek survived in early Christian literature (Hebrews 5–7), as also did the idea of an eschatological struggle between two opponents (Jude 9). However, these were never part of mainstream Christology, and Jesus was never called the true Melchizedek.

Jesus most probably knew some of these concepts, especially if John the Baptist, his teacher, shared some ideas with the Qumran community. Some of the Son of Man sayings obviously reflect a part of Jesus tradition which is parallel to his proclamation of the kingdom. In §2.1.3, we mentioned the saying from Q (Luke) 12:8–9 that also supposes a heavenly judgment as a dispute between two parties, one of them being the righteous guarantor of human hope. Here we have the idea which is most probably closest to Jesus' authentic hope. In that case, he considered himself to have a mission which certainly will be vindicated by God's representative in the eschatological struggle/trial. The Son of Man layer of the gospel tradition confirms that this concept was understandable at least for Palestinian Christians of Jewish origin. This is also why Psalm 110:1 ("Sit at my right hand") became so influential in the earliest Christology.

2.3.4 Jesus as the Davidic Messiah

Jesus was crucified as the "king of the Jews." This was the inscription of the charge on the cross (Mark 15:26; John 19:19–22) which, according to the Gospels, reflected the core of his cause (Mark 15:9, 12, 16ff., 32; John 18:33–34; 19:1–3, 12–15, 19–22). This may have originated from a one-sided interpretation of his trial, but, since the early Church avoided the title "king" for Jesus, it most probably was an interpretation originating from his contemporaries, especially from his adversaries. The context of mockery is still recognizable behind the tradition, even if the Gospel writers tried to cope with this offense by maintaining that, in fact, the adversaries paradoxically expressed the truth (see especially John 19:1–3).

Excursus: The Problem of Jesus' Descent and His Birthplace

One possible reason for identifying Jesus with the Davidic Messiah could have been his Davidic origin, as it is maintained by the infancy stories in the Gospels. The two stories in Luke (1:5 – 2:40) and in Matthew (1:1 – 2:23) are obviously of mutually independent origin. However, they are so different, that the only important information which may be valuable for our problem (i.e., the relationship between Jesus and the Christian Easter proclamation) is their quite narrow common denominator: a tendency to demonstrate the messianity of Jesus, especially to locate his birth to Bethlehem, the birthplace of David—the messianic king (Mic 5:1; Matt 2:5–6). Yet, this is just what is of interest for our investigation, and the infancy narratives may serve as a starting point for our argument, which will be derived from the inner coherence of several observations from the synoptic Jesus tradition.

The intent to support the post-Easter confession of Jesus' messianity must have preceded the formation of both the narratives about his nativity, yet it obviously was not the prevalent opinion prior to the crucifixion. In John 7:40–44, we read a tradition which has Jesus originating from Nazareth and which thus reveals some uncertainty in adopting the Bethlehem tradition in Early Christianity. In fact, both of the infancy narratives try to harmonize the two traditions. However, since the Davidide origin of Jesus is supposed in Rom 1:3–4, which is a pre-Pauline christological confession, it must have been quite an old tradition.

In the dialogue in Mark 12:35–37a, the problem is the relation between Jesus as Son of David and Jesus as Lord. If we combine this indirect evidence with the pericope on Peter's confession of Jesus as Messiah in Mark 8:29, we almost inevitably come to the conclusion that, at least in the expectation of some of his contemporaries, Jesus was indeed considered to be a messianic figure. The mighty argument against the post-Easter origin of this tradition is the terrible rebuke "Get behind me, Satan" addressed to Peter a few verses after his confession. In Matt 4:10, we read the same sentence addressed to the Satan himself after he has offered Jesus dominion over all the kingdoms of the world, i.e., the messianic power itself.

The wording of Peter's answer was quickly adapted according to the post-Easter confessions. It is visible in the Lukan (Luke 9:20) and especially in the Matthean version (Matt 16:16).

Jesus' proclamation of the kingdom as well as his solidarity with the poor may have been easily interpreted as messianic proclamation and messianic signs, as it is signaled in Q (Luke) 7:18–23. However, his absolute commandment of love (§2.1.3), as well as some of his symbolic actions (§2.2.3), reveal that he transformed some of the ideas which were customarily tied to the expectation of a Davidic Messiah. In light of these basic observations, the interpretation of Jesus as a revolutionary has to be abandoned.[65] If Jesus is to be called a revolutionary, it can only be in a metaphoric sense—a non-violent revolutionary.[66] It is obvious that the Davidic Messiah was expected to play a violent, military role, e.g., in the *Zadokite Document* (7:19–20: "... he shall smite all the children of Seth," cf. 1QM 11.6–7) or in Psalms of Solomon 17:21–25—all texts influenced by the oracle of Balaam from Numbers 24, which also inspired Rabbi Akiba to proclaim the militant revolutionary Bar Kokhba as Messiah.[67]

Jesus' response to the question about paying tribute to Caesar (attested in various versions in Mark 12:13–17; *GosThom* 100; or Papyrus Egerton 2 [2.14]) cannot be interpreted as a militant revolutionary attitude. This is reflected in the traditions on Christian relations with political power, respecting its relative legitimacy in the period prior to the eschatological change (Rom 13:1–7; 1 Pet 2:13–18; etc.). However, the criticism of Herodian and Roman power in Jesus tradition is undeniable (Luke 13:31ff.; Matt 20:25–27) and his proclamation of God's kingdom relativized political rule as well as the Mosaic Law.

2.3.5 The Death of Jesus

As we have mentioned (§2.2.5), the starting point of the charge against Jesus was probably his proclamation of a new, eschatological (and possibly spiritual) temple (Mark 14:58; John 2:19; cf. Acts 6:14). Since the Sanhedrin obviously did not possess the authority to pass the death penalty (John 18:31; *Jos bell* 2:117), Jesus, after the hearing described in the Gospels, was passed over to the Roman authorities, represented by Pilate, as a messianic pretender in the political sense.

The whole description is obviously influenced by apologetic intent, and the role of Roman authorities may have been more active than can be deduced from the canonical Gospels or from the *Gospel of Peter*. We have discussed the effect of Jesus' proclamation of the kingdom with all its universal consequences. The kingdom of God was a phenomenon with ecumenical and even cosmic dimensions, so that its anticipation must have, at least indirectly, also influenced the social and political balance of power in Palestine. Both the Jewish authorities in Jerusalem of that time (we have to stress: not "the Jews" and not all Jewish authorities) and the Roman power realized its possible impact in the area of their responsibility.

Jesus' sayings about the Temple obviously were only a pretext that enabled his adversaries to raise a charge against him.

But the fact that his activity aimed toward a deep change of their scale of values helps us to understand their rejection of Jesus as a consequence of their feeling that they were socially endangered.

The inner conflict that Jesus experienced during the last months and weeks of his life must have been very deep. His death on the cross put in question all hopes that were linked with his person and his mission.

2.3.6 Jesus Facing His Death

In the last months of his activity, Jesus must have realized the danger he was running. His sayings about drinking the cup and being baptized are metaphors of suffering (Mark 10:38–39; for the cup see Ps 75:9; Isa 51:17; *MartyrIsa* 5:13, for baptism see Ps 69:2–3) and may be a stylized pre-Easter expression of Jesus' self-understanding. We may trace here an eschatology and Christology similar to the Son of Man or Melchizedek imagery of eschatological struggle and subsequent proclamation (enthronement) of the victorious representative of God's justice and grace (§2.3.3). In favor of the pre-Easter origin is the fact that Jesus put the decision in the hands of God (and most of all the parallel in the Lukan special source, Luke 12:50): "I have to be baptized, and how I am constrained until it is completed!" A baptism that comes after the baptism of John is obviously the baptism by fire (Q [Luke] 3:16)—the apocalyptic suffering.

A special saying is the proverb "Whoever seeks to gain his life will lose it, but whoever loses his life will preserve it" from Q [Luke] 17:33, John 12:25, and a visibly post-Easter version in Mark 8:35. Originally, this was a proverb from military life: those who seek to survive by any means in battle, will die wretchedly, the courageous survive easier.[68] The Stoics transformed the moral import of the saying, as also did the Qumran people: In 1QM 7.5–6, we read about the warriors in the apocalyptic battle; they should be willing to face the hazards of battle; and, with such troops, the holy angels march. The multiple attestation makes it probable that Jesus knew such an aphorism and transformed it as consolation in his inner spiritual battle.[69]

Jesus' spiritual struggle obviously culminated soon before he was arrested and died on the cross.

The scene of the Last Supper in Mark 14:22–25; Luke 22:14–20; and 1 Cor 11:23–26 is clearly linked with the coming of the kingdom. It is its anticipation (Mark 14:25; Luke 22:16; 1 Cor 11:26—here the kingdom is "christologized" and expressed as Jesus' new coming). Obviously, Jesus considered his possible death to be a sacrifice that would open the way to the kingdom for other people, too. His comment on the bread as his body given (1 Cor 11:24) or the cup (as the wine) poured out "for you" (the participants of the meal) clearly expresses this opinion. Admittedly, the comment might have been reshaped in the post-Easter period with the help of Isa 53:4ff.—a Scripture quotation which was often used by Christians as a prophetic expression of the positive meaning of Jesus' death. However, even without the sayings, the gesture of offering the cup to the other participants (in Jewish meals everybody used his own cup) must have expressed the same thing. The original variety of meals with the risen Lord (real meals with bread and wine in 1 Cor 11:25, with bread only in Acts 2:46, with bread and fish in John 21:13, etc.) confirms the described intent of Jesus' meal fellowship.

A similar intent is revealed in the pericope on Jesus' prayer in Gethsemane (Mark 14:32–42; cf. John 12:27; Heb 5:7). In spite of its post-Easter narrative reshaping, it still bears traces of his inner struggle. He must have shared it with his disciples. The Church tried to decrease the scandal of Jesus' fear (in Matthew, Jesus did not pray that the "hour" might pass from him; in Luke 22, the majority of manuscripts left out verses 43–44 on the agony of Jesus, which are included in the Sinai Codex, Codex Bezae, and others). This all stresses the import of this scene, in which Jesus gave up all his ideas about the possible outcome of his story (e.g., ascension to heaven, bringing the kingdom before his death) and gave God the priority in deciding how to arrange the coming of his kingdom. His humble proclamation helped him to cope with the failure of his own expectations and ideas.

Dogmatic Excursus
On the surface, this seems to be an interpretation denying the Christian teaching about Jesus' divine nature. But, would Jesus be a real man, if he had known all? His life, his suffering, and his death were then parts of an—undeniably extremely difficult—actor's role. To say this would be a monofysitist heresy,

according to which Jesus was a God in human body. If Jesus represents God's will among humans, he must be a fully human being, who gradually realized his divine mission by identifying himself with God in a way appropriate to the humans—through inner growth and decision in his consciousness. This culminated in Gethsemane, where his union with God was realized through failure of his plans and ideas—in the moment when he gave them up. This is Jesus' union with God. Later this was formulated by means of Greek philosophical categories such as "nature" or "substance," which are quite static, so that they only express the intent of faith through paradoxical innovations (divine and human nature in one person).

Jesus' cry on the cross expressing his despair "My God, my God, why have you forsaken me?" (Mark 15:34) is in the present wording a quotation of Psalm 22 that ends with a positive expression of hope. The wording may be influenced by the tendency to legitimize Jesus' story. However, the tendency to produce new, more positive sayings pronounced on the cross (especially Luke 23:46 or John 19:30, "It is finished") is a clear evidence for Jesus' original despair. An independent evidence of this intent is the obviously Aramaic dialect of the version of Jesus' cry, its wording in the *Gospel of Peter* 19 ("My power, o power, you have forsaken me"—a later interpretation of the same tradition) and the reading of Mark 15:34 in Codex Bezae (". . . why have you /allow their having/ mocked me"—see Brown, 1994, § 42). Consequently, the interpretation in terms of Psalm 22 most probably is secondary: The cry on the cross expressed the deepest crisis of Jesus' life. Only the fact that he still does know the addressee with whom he may share his deepest sorrow and disillusion is the link between his earthly existence and the post-Easter Christian proclamation.

This extremely pious and liberal man of genius died on a cross, and all his excellence did not help him. The image of a dying wise man, who in his "noble death" becomes a model of the highest values, cannot be applied to Jesus in the oldest stratum of the passion story.

Christology

3.1 The Problem of a New Beginning

According to the classical Christian confessions, Easter was a new beginning, a new divine action of Jesus' resurrection which includes his rehabilitation by God himself. The phrase, "And all forsook him, and fled" (Mark 14:50) stressed the rupture between Jesus' earthly activity and the post-Easter proclamation. From a historical point of view, the rupture was not so deep, as can be seen in the Christian confessions. According to the Formula of Faith, the risen Jesus appeared to five hundred brothers at one time. In other words, his adherents were still gathering after his death.

If we want to discover the nature and meaning of Easter, we must start by discussing all those elements of early Christian history and theology which may relativize Easter and bypass it. We ought to be very hesitant to use categories like "unique" or "absolutely new."[1] On the other hand, we must not interpret the texts with a negative prejudice, supposing that they must be fully understandable from analogy, by comparison with other religious texts. This way we would miss the "new" which constitutes irreversible history.

The impact of John the Baptist, Jesus' contemporary, may be used as an argument for the post-mortal influence of a martyr. In such a case, an "Easter" may be superfluous. John's adherents survived in spite of their master's violent death, and up to the present time in Iraq there are several thousands of Mandeans—a semi-Jewish sect deriving its origin from his activity. Likewise, the violent death of the Righteous Teacher (Teacher of Righteousness; see §2.2.1) may have shocked his adherents, but at the same time it paradoxically increased his authority as the innocent martyr. The same is true of the suffering righteous one, similar to the "I" of several Psalms (22, 69, 70, 71, 73, 74, etc.). Admittedly, the post-mortal influence in these cases did not evoke any significant missionary activity, as happened in the case of Jesus.

We shall not discuss the obviously one-sided hypotheses which maintain that the Jesus' followers spread a false message about his resurrection in order that they might affect society to their own favor. Such hypotheses appear from the earliest period: In the second century, the Platonic philosopher Celsus wrote "The True Teaching," in which he interpreted the resurrection of Jesus as an invention. Others maintained that Jesus' death was an illusion.[2] It has even been suggested that Jesus' post-resurrection appearances were nothing more than hallucinogenic visions induced by eating mushrooms. All these hypotheses ignore both the facts and the nature of the texts and produce more problems than they attempt to solve. How could such an imaginary event have evoked the rise of Christianity?

3.1.1 The Christology of Jesus' Sacrificial Death

We have already mentioned the interpretation of Jesus' death as a substitutive sacrifice, as in the phrase "for our sins" (or "for us") in the Formula of Faith (1 Cor 15:3; see §1.2.4–5). We have demonstrated that this interpretation is included in the institution of the Lord's Supper (§2.3.6) and that it represents a link between the pre- and post-Easter tradition. It is possible that Jesus' adherents celebrated the Eucharist in their master's memory (1 Cor 11:24b, 25b) as a repeated anticipation of the coming kingdom of God. In this respect, the Christology of the sacrificial death of Jesus was meaningful by itself.

At the same time, we must consider that the new supposition that Jesus was present among the participants as the Lord (§3.3.1.3) must have been evoked by a new and positive experience with Jesus.

3.1.2 Christology of the Son of Man

Another Christology that may have not been evoked by Easter is the Son of Man Christology, or, better formulated, the expression of Jesus' significance by identifying him with the apocalyptic Son of Man. We understand that for some of his adherents, especially among Aramaic-speaking Jews, the expectation of his new coming with power as the Son of Man must have been a source of hope. The crucified was expected to return and judge his judges (cf. Mark 14:62).

The problem is to prove the existence of such an expectation as a separate stream. The oldest document of a similar apocalyptic expectation is the short Aramaic prayer "Maranatha" (1 Cor 16:22; *Did* 10:5; cf. Rev 22:20). Theoretically, it could be interpreted as a prayer for the reappearance of Jesus as the teacher, as the Lord in the sense of a Rabbi. But the Aramaic title Lord (*mārēʾ*) occurs in Dan 5:23 (cf. 2:47) for God. This is supported by new evidence from Qumran.[3] Consequently, the title was not a secular designation such as Rabbi, but an honorific title, and there must have been some new impulse which caused its introduction by a group of Jesus' adherents after his crucifixion. When his post-Easter adherents identified him as the Lord, or as the Son of God, they may have used some of his own ideas. However, the full identification must have been a bold decision supposing his exaltation. Otherwise, Jesus would never have become the addressee of a prayer like "Maranatha." The coming Lord is the *Kyrios* (Lord) of Christian post-Easter confessions (1 Cor 11:26), the Son of God who has been raised (1 Thess 1:10).

3.1.3 Wisdom Christology

The literary source of the sayings of Jesus (Q) is a hypothetical document which explains the common material in Matthew and Luke which is not in the Gospel of Mark. The most important document supporting the existence and importance of collections of sayings, such as Q must have been, is the *Gospel of Thomas*—a collection of 114 sayings of Jesus, which had been known in a small fragment only until a Coptic translation was discovered among the Nag Hammadi texts.[4] Having this in mind we may identify a group of other later writings as belonging to this genre, e.g., the *Book of Thomas, the Contender*,[5] the

Dialog of the Savior,[6] and, in a broader sense, the *Gospel of Philip,*[7] the *Secret Book of John,*[8] and dialogues such as *Pistis Sophia,*[9] etc.

The oldest indirect evidence is the sayings of the Lord in Paul's letters (1 Cor 7:10; 9:14; or 1 Thess 4:15). He obviously quoted them from some collection of the Lord's sayings by which they were handed.

In Q, Jesus is identified with wisdom (Q [Luke] 7:35; 11:31). Because of this, several scholars suppose that the group which created this collection considered him to be the living wisdom.

Unlike the other alternative Christologies, the wisdom Christology can be associated with its typical literary genre, which survived at least till the end of the second century as an autonomous group inside the Christianity.

The *Gospel of Thomas,* with its visibly Gnostic tendency, recognizable in the preserved wording of more then one-third of the sayings, illustrates clearly why this genre has been abandoned by the Church: Without the frame of Jesus' life and death, it was easily used by overenthusiastic followers (and later by Gnostic groups) to develop new interpretations that were different from the intent of the mainstream Church. This is why the theory of Jesus as a teacher of wisdom, similar to the Cynics,[10] gained ground, at least among a small but influential group of scholars.

On the other hand, it must be admitted that, from the earliest period, collections of Jesus' sayings also belonged to the tradition of groups that accepted the resurrection Christology: The apostle Paul is fully dependent on the resurrection Christology, as we have demonstrated in our analysis of the Formula of Faith from 1 Cor 15:3b–5, and he knew a collection of Jesus' sayings. He undoubtedly had some reservations about this genre of collected wise sayings (in 1 Cor 1:22, he warned of the "Greeks" [= Hellenistic Christians?] predilection for wisdom). However, in some instances, the sayings of Jesus was apparently his decisive authority.

We have pointed out that Matthew integrated the Q into his Gospel, as did Luke. Both also used the Gospel of Mark, which is deeply influenced by the Pauline Christology of cross and resurrection. This suggests that these two documents (Q and Mark) did not represent two different and alternative Christologies, but rather two different dimensions of the liturgical life of the same group.

3.1.4 Conclusions

(a) In spite of obvious continuity, our observations confirmed that a new experience arose between the death of Jesus and the earliest Christian statements.

(b) We discovered an integrative ability of the resurrection/exaltation Christology, i.e., it was meaningful to many different groups of Christians and gradually became the orthodox view. This does not mean that there were not other streams. When J. Z. Smith (1990) speaks of the Early Christianities in the plural, he rightly describes the great variety of Christian groups of the first century, but he ignores the integrative power of certain theological concepts, which made Christianity very different in both spiritual and social terms, from the other religions of Late Antiquity.

(c) The oldest Christologies (or christological elements), which we may only reconstruct or assume (Son of Man Christology, wisdom Christology, the suffering righteous Christology, etc.) are not necessarily the best ones—they do not necessarily correspond to the initial event in the best way. In most new movements, the beginnings are experimental. Only after a short period of experiments do people find the proper expression of an experience that mediates a new reality. This was the case also with the resurrection event, which changed the course of human spirituality and culture. The integration of Christologies started so soon that the alternatives which we have been able to deduce are historically verifiable only to a very limited extent.

(d) The variety and high claim (Jesus is proclaimed to be the person who is decisive for human salvation) of the early Christologies confirms that the source of Christian christological reflection was not mere speculation, but must have been some event that evoked these various reactions. An artificial construct, deliberately fabricated, would have been more consequential and less open to different interpretations.

(e) Therefore, our task in investigating early Christologies is to interpret their function and the way they became compatible with other concepts, especially with the resurrection/exaltation Christology which proved to become the focus of christological reflection. We have to ask what was the reason for this integrative ability of the resurrection/exaltation Christology and why were some of the earliest Christologies incompatible with it, so that they were eventually either excluded or reinterpreted through incorporation into new created literary units and genres. To sum up: The Early Christian Christologies "behave" like a system consisting of various different elements (subsystems) which in different ways reflects one mighty impulse.[11]

3.2 Easter

According to the Formula of Faith, Jesus' post-resurrection appearances must have taken place soon after the resurrection itself, which is said to be the "third day" after the death of Jesus. The "third day" is undoubtedly influenced by the biblical expectation of God's acting on the third day (Gen 22:4; Exod 19:11; cf. Hos 6:2). Paul considered his encounter with the risen Lord, which happened much later, to be of the same kind as the other Easter appearances (1 Cor 15:8–9).

The sentences on Jesus' resurrection do not speak about the resurrection itself, they proclaim it only, obviously in all cases on the basis of its consequences, i.e., the appearances of Jesus as the risen Lord. It is only the *Gospel of Peter* (second century) that describes the resurrection itself.

The Christians who promulgated and adopted the resurrection/exaltation Christology had no forceful means of supporting their view other than their own testimony. As with every situation in which coincident testimony is offered by numerous people, the testimony about Jesus' resurrection has to be taken seriously even by a non-Christian scholar.

3.2.1 Resurrection Christology

The content of the vision is not easy to define. However, it confirmed an unexpected presence of Jesus in a new status. In the narratives on his appearances as the risen Lord, this is expressed by the motif of non-recognition (Matt 28:17b; Luke 24:16;

John 21:4). This motif is present even when his words and actions reveal his personal identity.

The category "resurrection" is an interpretation produced by the witnesses. Since Jesus proclaimed the kingdom of God, it is probable that the witnesses of the first appearances supposed that he already participated in the kingdom, that he already shared the new existence, which, according to the dominant apocalyptic stream, should be introduced by a general resurrection. This was a bold innovation of the apocalyptic view (see §1.2.3). The resurrection of Jesus was separated from the resurrection of other people, and the eschatology (and in fact the hope) was split into two poles:

(a) The resurrection of Jesus was the present guarantee of eschatological fulfillment, which was linked with an attested event in the past, so that the earthly life of the risen Lord could be kept in "memory." The Messiah has been revealed. However, it is only he himself who has already entered the age to come.

(b) This means that there is also the second pole—the future fulfillment itself, the coming of the kingdom of God in power, or—in the post-Easter terminology: Jesus' second coming in power—the salvation.

This can be demonstrated from the oldest written document of Christianity, the first letter of Paul to the Thessalonians (1:9b–10), where the author reminds the addressees that through their conversion they ". . . turned from idols to God, to serve a living and true God [the monotheistic phase of conversion common for Jews and Christians] and to wait for his Son from heaven [the second pole of Christian hope from a christological point of view], whom he raised from the dead." Jesus is the first pole, who rescues us from the wrath that is coming (the second pole from a soteriological point of view).

The fact that the christological statement of Jesus' resurrection implied a bipolar eschatology and soteriology was an important step for Christian theology. It created a pattern described as the "doubled eschatology" by the Czech scholar J. B. Souček in 1932. In the current theology, it is often called "telescopic eschatology." This is a phenomenon of great impact not only in Christian theology, but also in Western culture as a whole.

Ernst Käsemann was right when he said that apocalyptic was the mother of Christian theology.[12] This does not mean that Christian faith was born from apocalyptic, it means only that theology developed by transforming the apocalyptic ideas of its Jewish setting which were present also in Jesus' own proclamation. This is why the post-Easter adherents of Jesus proclaimed their Easter visions to be a consequence of Jesus' resurrection. This means that Easter has proclaimed a part of the eschatological fulfillment, of the age to come.

The telescopic eschatology was so integrative because, in a simple way, it expressed the complex experience of the first Christians. The groups whose Christology concentrated only on the expected fulfillment, i.e., on Jesus' second coming, as well as those who in an enthusiastic way concentrated on the presence of the Lord in wisdom or in spirit, were unable to survive as groups. In fact, such groups have reappeared again and again, but they have been parasites of the resurrection Christology, which made their existence possible.

3.2.1.1 An Individual Reanimation?

From the very beginning, Easter was interpreted as an individual reanimation of Jesus, in nearly the same sense as by those people who considered him to be John the Baptist raised from the dead (Mark 6:14; cf. 8:28). This was used by several scholars as an argument in favor of an alternative Christology, which G. H. C. Macgregor called "reanimation" in 1939. However, there are several facts that prevent us from considering these motifs to be an alternative Christology:

(a) Independent testimonies speak of Jesus' presence after Easter as a transformed one.

(b) Easter evoked an enthusiastic movement, which was interpreted as the eschatological period of Spirit (see below §3.2.3).

(c) Individual reanimation was also a part of the apocalyptic drama, as in Rev 11:7–13, where the two reanimated prophets initiate the apocalyptic cosmic drama (cf. Matt 27:52–53).

(d) In the oldest letter of Paul, 1 Thessalonians, Easter is closely linked with apocalyptic expectation.

3.2.2 The Exaltation of Jesus

From the beginning, the resurrection has also been viewed as an elevation or exaltation (Rom 1:3–4; Mark 12:36, as it was with the Messiah/Son of Man tradition according to *1 Enoch* 51:3; cf. 45:3–6; 71:5–17; *Jubilees* 4:21). Psalm 110:1 has played a role in this interpretation of Easter. "Above" is in all cultures the key position. Elevation is an expression of the positive character of Easter that is understandable in itself, but does not exclude the role of the Messiah in the eschatological (apocalyptic) fulfillment, as we discussed in §1.2.3.

There were, no doubt, alternative interpretations of the exaltation. They are indirectly attested by the fact that Paul considers it necessary to mention all those Christians who proclaim (their faith) this way (1 Cor 15:11). Those who "denied the resurrection" (1 Cor 15:12) were obviously expressing their faith another way.

One possibility is that they did not accept the present dimension of salvation and expected the near coming of the kingdom. They did not expect resurrection from death, since they expected a transformation of all to take place very soon. This would have been something like the expectation we encounter in 1 Thess 4:13, where Paul addressed the problem of those who died before the second coming of Christ, and who thus, in the mind of the Thessalonians, had lost their chance of entering the new age.

However, there is another solution that is more probable. It supposes that Paul's opponents did not expect a resurrection since they had experienced it already in a spiritual way. In 1 Cor 4:6–13, we read about Corinthian Christians who disdained earthly labor (4:12) and considered themselves kings, wise and rich, so that Paul had to stress the "not yet" of Christian hope and make them aware of God's coming judgment. This was probably the group that denied the resurrection in 1 Corinthians 15. According to them, salvation had already taken place (cf. 2 Tim 2:17–18), since they experienced it spiritually.[13]

3.2.3 The Character of the Easter Experience

The enthusiastic interpretation of Easter in the sense of the full presence of salvation is the most important alternative of mainstream resurrection Christology. It has traditionally been viewed as nothing more than a side effect of Christian proclamation, but what we observe in the Corinthian correspondence reveals it as the original and immediate reaction to Easter. Throughout history, this reaction reappeared several times and has kept its appeal up to the present.

This enthusiastic reaction to Easter is expressed by fragments of the opinions of Paul's adversaries, who understood Easter enthusiasm as a kind of drunkenness (Acts 2:13, 15; Eph 5:18–20) or even madness (1 Cor 14:23; cf. Acts 26:24–25).

The post-Easter visions provide indirect information about the cause of such a reaction. The most dramatic content of the visions was a light (Acts 9:3; 22:6; 26:13—Paul's encounter with the risen Lord; Mark 9:3; 2 Pet 1:16–17—Jesus' transfiguration; Rev 1:13–16). This is confirmed by several Gnostic texts from Nag Hammadi where the risen Christ is associated with light, such as in the letter of Peter to Philip.[14]

Light is a symbol of God,[15] God's presence (Exod 13:21–22; Ps 104:2; Hab 3:4; Dan 2:22), and God's revelation (Isa 9:1–2; Matt 4:16; 17:2). The post-Easter experience of light was therefore considered to be divine.

In this context, light signifies a positive character of the appearances. This is evidenced also by numerous instances in which Easter enthusiasm was linked with joy, as in 2 Cor 8:2; 1 Pet 1:8; Luke 24:52–53; Acts 2:26; Rev 19:6b–8; cf. Matt 5:12; Jude 24. It is understandable that such an experience was understood as an ultimate, absolute sign of Jesus' rehabilitation by God, as a sign of his new presence, a presence no less real than his temporal body—a presence through which the proclaimed kingdom of God penetrated into this age.

3.3 From Easter to its Various Expressions

The enthusiastic expression of the Easter experience was soon augmented or replaced by reflected statements. Any authentic enthusiasm soon has to be transformed into a verbalized information. In an earlier book,[16] I used an analogy of the story of a mother whose son was in a battle during the war and had not received any news about him for a long time. Suddenly, somebody rings the bell, she opens the door, and the son is there and embraces her. Her first reaction is not the most rational one; she feels an overwhelming joy, they are dancing and crying, and the tears of joy are accompanied by shouts lacking any logic, like "Is it really you?" So Luke wrote about reactions to the appearances of the risen Lord in Jerusalem: "And they still disbelieved for joy, and wondered . . ." (Luke 24:41).

This period of joy was rightly conserved liturgically, but it also had to be verbalized and reflected upon as soon as possible. This was a necessary second step. Otherwise, the movement might have remained limited to those who experienced the original event, or it might have lost its identity and become mixed with enthusiasm of different origin, or it could even have disappeared altogether. So it is with the mother in our story, too. If she had remained in the first reaction for more then (in their case) four or five minutes, her enthusiasm would be considered to be rather an expression of hysteria than a response to a wonderful experience. Her next step should be to pass on the information: "Mary, come, John is here!" or such.

Unlike the case of the mother, the content of Easter was not visible or readily perceptible. It was experienced as an encounter with a signal of the age to come, i.e., in modern terms, with transcendence. It follows that the verbalization had to be shaped as a testimony directed to other humans, and as an acclamation directed toward God as the initiator of Jesus' new presence.

Reflection on the event can be considered the third step, as if the mother in our story would say: "This means that in my old age we shall have help, since John will take care of us." Her reflection is a very elementary and self-evident one. However, because the encounter with transcendence could be expressed only by analogy, in a metaphoric way, it is very difficult to separate reflection from verbalization.

Thus, the verbalization of Easter as Jesus' resurrection includes a good deal of reflection. Since the Easter experience is of a transcendent nature, Jesus' new presence must be the eschatological one, belonging to the age to come. And since the new age has not yet arrived, Jesus in his resurrection is its precursor. He opens the universal and absolute future—his death and his new presence are not only a happy end to his personal story, they open salvation for all. The news of his resurrection is good news.

In a later period, the reflection addressed further problems:

(a) What will be the role of Jesus in the period of universal fulfillment? (A second coming in power, his positive role during the last judgment, the coming of the kingdom of God, etc. See, e.g., 1 Cor 15:25–28. In sum, this is Christian eschatology.)

(b) How should we, in light of Easter, cope with the past? What is the meaning of the cosmos as God's creation? (Creation is the realm of revelation of God's glory and God's good will in Jesus, so that he must have been preexistent, preceding even the process of creation [1 Cor 8:6; Col 1:15–20; Heb 1:1–3 and later evidence], etc.; short: Christian **protology**.) In this context, wisdom Christology, which was associated with the idea of preexistent wisdom (Prov 8:22–31),[17] acquired a new function: to express the irrevocable validity of Jesus who has been raised from dead.

(c) What does it mean that Easter is the revelation of God's full will and intention? (Jesus is the "only" Son of God [John 3:16]—there is no other who will reveal other features of God's will. This is Christian soteriology, etc.)

With these notes, we can already anticipate the later developments. Here we have to stress the importance of such reflections in the development of the Easter proclamation. Although we have agreed with Käsemann that apocalypticism was the mother of Christian theology, we have to modify this slightly by saying that it was transformed apocalypticism, based upon reflection on the Easter event, that was the mother of Christian theology.

3.3.1 Christological Titles and Confessional Sentences
Another useful approach to investigating Jesus' significance after his crucifixion is to examine the christological titles and confessional sentences.

3.3.1.1 Christ
We have already mentioned (§2.3.1) that Jesus accepted the messianic expectations, as far as they were linked with his

person, with reluctance. It is thus a matter of interest that even the oldest post-Easter texts consider him to be the Messiah (Christ) without any hesitation. Such formulae are well attested: "He (Jesus) is the Messiah," as in Mark 8:29; Acts 9:22; 17:3; John 7:41; 1 John 5:1.[18] It is therefore clear that something must have happened after his crucifixion that enabled his adherents to formulate such a confession.

That it was not formulated according to a given messianic expectation may be deduced from the fact that often the title Messiah was linked with proclamation of his death or suffering (Rom 5:6; Gal 2:21; 3:13; 1 Pet 3:18; Acts 3:18–19; 17:3; 26:23). This was a striking transformation of contemporary messianic ideas, but only a transformation. The earliest Christian groups of Jesus adherents were, at least for a transitory period, a Jewish messianic movement.

It is possible that Jesus' identification with the messianic king (Messiah, Christ) was provoked by the inscription on his cross "The King of the Jews/Israel" (Mark 15:26, cf. John 19:19). That the identification of Jesus with Messiah occurred shortly after Easter may be supported by the following observation: In Paul's time, the title Christ was common, so common and self-evident that it was understandable to most of the readers of his letters (and in practice turned into a second name of Jesus), while John (writing later) had to explain it to his readers (John 1:41). In sum: The title Christ means that, for Christians, messianic expectations are focused on Jesus.

3.3.1.2 Son of Man
See §2.3.3 for a discussion of this title.

3.3.1.3 Kyrios (Lord)
We have already mentioned the bold decision to call Jesus Lord and the two dimensions of the title Lord as applied to Jesus: The first is the Aramaic invocation (prayer) "Our Lord, come!" (1 Cor 16:22; 1 Thess 2:19; etc.; cf. "The Lord is at hand," Phil 4:5; see §3.1.2), and the second is the acclamation "Jesus (is) Lord" (1 Cor 12:3). From Phil 2:6–11 and Rom 10:9, we may deduce that the acclamation of Jesus as the Lord was a central part of the liturgy. Several scholars[19] have maintained that these two Lord titles are of different origin and that they have

different functions. In fact, the two ways of using the title Lord simply reflect the bipolarity of Christian post-Easter (telescopic) eschatology, as represented in resurrection Christology (§3.2.1). Their common denominator is the present attainability of the risen Lord—as the addressee of prayers as well as the object of acclamation.

3.3.1.4 Son of God

"Son of God" replaced the title Messiah (Christ) in the identifying confessions (Mark 1:11; Matt 14:33; Acts 9:20; John 1:49; 1 John 4:15; 5:5; etc.; cf. Q [Luke] 4:3, 9). This transition is still visible in Matt 16:16 (cf. Mark 8:29), where both titles are combined.

Originally, the title was derived from Jewish messianic expectations, especially those related to Ps 2:6–8 (cf. Ps 89:27–28 [LXX = 88]) and to 2 Sam 7:14, where God calls David's descendant his son. Pharisaic monotheism oppressed these traditions, but from Qumran we have evidence that they were still alive in Jesus' time: In an anthology of eschatological texts from the Scripture,[20] 2 Sam 7:14 is quoted as messianic text, and in the Aramaic *Pseudo-Daniel*,[21] the messianic figure is called Son of God.[22] The popularity of the title Son of God is documented by the Son formula in Rom 1:3–4, where it is linked with the motif of resurrection (as in 1 Thess 1:9–10) and by its occurrence in the so-called formulae of sending (Gal 4:4–5; Rom 8:3–4; John 3:17; 1 John 4:9; cf. John 3:16; etc.).[23]

The rapid spread of the title was partially due to the fact that it was understandable even in a pagan setting, where several heroes were considered to be sons of deities. These were, of course, misinterpretations, and the Christians had to interpret the new function of the term (Rom 5:10; Mark 15:39).

The main advantage of the title is its ability to express the impact of Easter: We know already that the experience of Jesus' helplessness on the cross was considered to be a part of his substitutional death. However, it was necessary to indicate at least indirectly that the death of Jesus as God's representative did not create a crisis (in our contemporary terminology the "death") of God himself. God was the counterpart and the giver of salvation even to his dying Son. This was the unexpressed, but actually functioning, advantage of the title Son of God. Jesus

represented God as a human being who was dependent on salvation coming from God himself—as the Son of God.

All that we have said so far in this section reveals an explo-
sion of christological titles soon after Jesus' death. The fact that
they became so deeply interwoven with each other and with
various Christologies (resurrection, exaltation, second coming,
suffering, etc.), does not exclude the existence of different christological concepts, but it puts these differences in perspective.

3.3.2 The Q Source[24]

It is not easy to discover the general literary pattern of Q as a
whole—just as difficult as with other collections of sayings.
There are smaller clusters of sayings that have been gathered
according to a key term. However, it is very probable that Q was
a literary unit, since some parts show literary consistency. On
the other hand, in some instances the differences are so striking
(e.g., Q [Luke] 19:12–27; cf. Matt 25:14–30, the Parable of the
Talents) that some scholars have asked whether Q was not sub-
stantially shorter than the "double tradition," (i.e., than the
material common to Luke and Matthew which is not in Mark).
They suggest that Q may include only those units with literary
agreement.[25]

Theologically, the most important feature of Q is the
absence of a passion story. In fact, the presence of a passion
story would not fit the genre of a collection of sayings. Together
with the absence of the title Christ, this is a finding of theological significance. Q is, in fact, a Jewish text dealing with the
theology of Jesus and was only indirectly and additionally influenced by Easter.[26] The Christology of Q was that of Jesus as the
always valid and therefore living wisdom (see Q [Luke] 7:35;
11:31), as we have discussed in §3.1.3.

A possible objection is that Q also includes some eschatological warnings typical of prophecy (Q [Luke] 11:39–52,
etc.).[27] Since, according to Luke 11:49 (obviously Q), it is wisdom that sends the prophets, this difference of genres is not so
important. Its weight would increase if it were possible to prove
that the prophetic sayings are a later addition, sometimes called
Q^2.[28] However, this is a controversial stratification.[29]

The main christological features of Q are:

(a) Jesus' relation to John the Baptist, whose expectation of the "more powerful one" is applied to Jesus (Q [Luke] ch. 3 and 7:18–35).

(b) eschatological expectation immediately affecting the present (13:20–21; Lord's Prayer, 11:2–4).

(c) the commandment of love in its absolute intention (love of enemies), proclaimed as the main duty—a reaction to the unconditioned promise of salvation for the poor and for the sinners.[30] As messenger of God's kingdom Jesus is the founder of a new interpretation of Law and of a new moral.

(d) the suffering of the Jewish community and the failures of Jewish politics are interpreted as a consequence of Israel's inner failure (the so-called deuteronomistic view of history. See, e.g., 2 Chr 30:7–8); on the other hand, the coming kingdom will include pagans as its full members (Q [Luke] 13:28–30; cf. §2.1.2).

If we consider Q as an isolated textual unit, it undeniably represents a special Christology, different from resurrection Christology. The polemics against those who prefer wisdom to the cross of Jesus in 1 Cor 1:22 indirectly confirms the existence of groups that could have represented the Christology of Q.

No doubt, such a group did exist within the Christian community in Corinth, but this does not mean that it shared the resurrection Christology of the majority of Corinthian Christians. The Nag Hammadi texts offer a later evidence of Gnostic polemic against these other Christians. It is clear from these texts that the Gnostics, in criticizing Christian authorities,[31] as well as the adoration of a dead man (i.e., the crucified Jesus),[32] belonged to the Christian community and considered themselves to be its spiritual elite, neglected by the others, and yet serving them by their witness to a higher, exclusively spiritual Savior.[33]

Until Ireneus of Lyon (the end of the second century), the oral tradition of Jesus' sayings was alive in the Church and obviously coexisted with the resurrection Christology and with literary genres like the canonical Gospels. It is possible that Q and its Christology originated as a complementary part of the liturgical life of several Christian communities.[34] In that case, the *Gospel of Thomas* and other later collections of sayings would represent a proto-Gnostic stream of interpretation, whereas the incorporation of Q and similar anthologies in the canonical scriptures (e.g., Luke) were a logical consequence of its interpretation in terms of resurrection Christology.

3.3.2.1 The Nag Hammadi Texts and Our Problem

In this context, the *Gospel of Thomas* plays a very important role: It enables us to reconstruct the origins of other Christian literary traditions which claim to mediate a direct communication with the Living Christ and which, as to genre, consist of sayings collections and dialogues (e.g., the *Dialogue with the Savior*[35]). The *Gospel of Thomas* and other Nag Hammadi texts of this kind illustrate the specific affinity of Gnostic interpretation for this alternative christological tradition.

Another Gnostic influence may be seen in one of the basic variants of the Redeemer Myth (§1.2.5 Excursus), as documented by Phil 2:6–11 and the two texts quoted in Col 1:15–20 and Eph 2:14–17a. All of them describe the work of Jesus as redeemer in a cosmic context and suppose his preexistence. This image could be derived from Gnostic myths dealing with the fall of the heavenly Man into the material world.[36] Since the oldest formulae do not mention the preexistent Jesus, we have to consider the idea of Jesus as the cosmic redeemer to be of non-Pauline, but not necessarily pre-Pauline origin. However, Paul and his followers reinterpreted the pre-Gnostic ideas relating to preexistence and exaltation Christology.

3.3.3 The Passion Narrative

The passion story is the central literary unit of the canonical Gospels as well as of the *Gospel of Peter*. This led the German scholar Karl L. Schmidt to a general statement that the Gospel of Mark (as the first representative of this literary subgenre) is in fact a passion story with an expanded preface.[37] However, new research has posed some crucial questions which may change this image: Did the passion story exist before Mark? And how can the Christologies of the passion story relate to resurrection Christology?

Some scholars maintain that a pre-Markan passion story did not exist.[38] It is true that a pre-Markan passion narrative cannot be reconstructed as a literary unit. On the other hand, the fact that Mark's theology is mostly different from the recognizable Christologies of the individual parts of the passion story supports the assumption of pre-Markan origins of individual passion traditions. It is also very probable that the different Christologies of the individual parts of the passion story were not considered to be contradictory and that they represented a collection of oral traditions when Mark took them over.

If we look at the most influential elements of the passion narrative (Mark 14:1 – 16:8, according to the most ancient manuscripts), we clearly recognize the Anointing at Bethany (14:3–9), the Passover with Disciples (14:12–26), and the Resurrection of Jesus (16:1–8) as units with a high degree of independence. The tradition on Peter's Denial (14:27–31 and 66–72) is interwoven with the story of Jesus before the Council in such a sophisticated literary manner that we must consider it to be most probably a work of Mark.

We may discern several other subunits within the bulk of the Markan passion narrative (The Arrest of Jesus; Jesus before the Council; Jesus before Pilate; The Mocking, Crucifixion, and Death of Jesus; and The Burial), but these traditions have been transmitted with a common denominator:

(a) All the main segments of the narrative of Jesus' trial and death (Mark 14:24, 27, 50) are part of an apocalyptic drama which allude to Zech 9:11; 13:7; and 14:5. Matthew and John noticed this and added further allusions to Zechariah. In this drama, the striking of the shepherd and the final victory of God are parts of the same movement. The cry of the dying Jesus in darkness is interpreted as the voice of God, the Lord, proclaiming his reestablished reign on Zion based on Joel 4:15–16. The tearing of the temple curtain is the beginning of a period of a new eschatological temple (1 Enoch 90:28–29), or of the age to come with its direct access to God and with no temple at all. We observe that the scriptural support covers the whole range of traditions. The structure of the passion narrative is more an expression of Jesus' role in salvation, than reflection on his biographical data.[39] The climax of the trial—the dialogue with the high priest (the language of which is non-Markan)—is also apocalyptic. Jesus mentions the coming of the Son of Man as his vindication. The Son of Man, in the sense of the proclaimer of

God's eschatological judgment (Dan 7:13), is declared to be identical with Jesus (cf. a similar tradition in John 9:35ff.). This set of arguments from Scripture is obviously pre-Markan and so, most probably, are the narrative units bound by it into a comprehensive unit. Mark, as a personality intending a synthesis, respected the theology of the passion narrative as he found it when he started to write his Gospel, and he even developed it. But he did so under the auspices of resurrection Christology, which was linked with a christological interpretation of Jesus' death as a sacrifice for human sins. This was the Christology he learned from the Formula of Faith (§1.2.3).

(b) The apocalyptic intent of the passion narrative does not correspond to the theology of Mark, who focuses on Jesus' sacrificial death and his vindication through resurrection. Isaiah 53, with verses 8 and 12 as the main scriptural arguments for the sacrificial death of Jesus, is quoted, but only as an interpretation of Jesus' silence during his trial (Isa 53:7 in Mark 14:61a). I should not need to say that the Christology of the Son of Man is different from the main Markan christological intention, even though Mark tried to integrate it. When, in Mark 14:62, Jesus reminds the high priest of the eschatological coming of the Son of Man as the agent of God, he, in fact, proclaims a divine judgment over his judges. We have already discussed the evidence for Jesus' expectation of the last judgment as a dispute between two parties, one of them being the righteous guarantor of hope and salvation (Q [Luke] 12:8; see §2.3.3). This saying of Jesus must be considered the apex of this expectation, which does not suppose resurrection Christology.

(c) Additional evidence for the presence of pre-Markan units in the passion narrative is the information given in Mark 14:43 that Judas was one of the Twelve, which is well known to those who read Mark's Gospel as whole (see Mark 3:19; 14:10!). How extensive the pre-Markan text was is difficult to say. However, the likelihood of its existence is very probable.[40]

(d) That the passion narrative was a stabilized oral tradition before Mark integrated it into his Gospel, can be supported also by investigating the **lexical** means linking the passion traditions with each other, i.e., by the function of the verb "to hand over" ("to betray") which in Greek is *paradidonai*.[41] Jesus is betrayed by Judas to the temple police (Mark 14:44) like a criminal (Acts 8:3), then to Pilate (Mark 15:1), then to the soldiers for crucifixion (15:15). In sum: Jesus as the Son of Man is betrayed into the hands of sinners (14:41). However, the eschatological appearance of the Son of Man will be his vindication, by God himself (14:62)—his final victory and the judgment of his judges. This eschatological rehabilitation is expected as a counterpart of human sinful activity. All of the verses cited above (except Mark 14:62) employ the same verb, *paradidonai.* In this way, the passion traditions have been integrated into a single narrative. The individual motifs were pre-Easter, the integration obviously post-Easter, but pre-Markan. This may be deduced from the fact that Markan interpretations of the passion narrative focus on the Christology of resurrection (9:31; 10:33–34), whereas, in the pre-Markan story, the apex was the expected eschatological vindication of Jesus at the threshold of the age to come (14:62). After Easter, this tradition was transformed only through the fact that the expected Lord was considered as the addressee of present prayers, as we have seen in the invocation Maranatha (see §3.1.2).

(e) The short Pauline comment on the passion of Jesus in 1 Cor 11:23–26 supposes that the passion narrative was already linked with the institution of the Lord's Supper, i.e., with a sacrificial interpretation of his death as a substitutive one (see §3.1.1). On the other hand, it is very improbable that at that time the passion narrative already included the pericope of the Empty Tomb (Mark 16:1–8), since Paul would use it as argument in 1 Cor 15:12–13, 35ff., 47–49, 52–54 in confirming the proclamation of Jesus' resurrection. According to Paul's anthropology, resurrection meant that the mortal body would be replaced by a new one by the Creator's activity. According to 1 Cor 15:42ff., Paul must have supposed that Jesus' tomb was empty, but he did not know the tradition of the open tomb. This means that he supposed the resurrection of the crucified Jesus, as he has proclaimed it, but he did know the passion narrative in a version which was not yet shaped by resurrection Christology.

It is significant that, in 1 Cor 11:26, we find the same expectation of the Savior's coming at the end of this age, as in the passion narrative in Mark 14:62. Even the betrayal motif is present here in verse 23. Since, in the Formula of Faith, the Christology of Jesus' sacrificial death is closely associated with the Christology of resurrection, both these Christologies, as well as the Christology of the Son of Man, must have been considered to be complementary expressions of Easter in Pauline Christian communities in the 50s, i.e., twenty years before Mark's Gospel.

In sum, the passion narrative undoubtedly represents a Christology different from that of Jesus' sacrificial death as well as from the Christology of resurrection. However, in the time and setting of Mark's Gospel, they were not considered alternatives, so that Mark, in composing his Gospel, only consummated the inherent tendency of his liturgical setting toward integration of various post-Easter Christologies.

Recently, several scholars have suggested that the passion story according to the apocryphal *Gospel of Peter* may be an independent witness of the earliest tradition. The *Gospel of Peter* is a fragment consisting only of the incomplete passion narrative. It represents a Christology of miraculous vindication of Jesus with a vivid depiction of Jesus' crucifixion and—unlike the canonical Gospels—of his resurrection. Jesus, leaving the tomb, is seen by a whole company of Roman soldiers, his figure reaches to the heavens, etc. According to these scholars, the miraculous elements have been suppressed in Mark, under the influence of Pauline theology.[42] It is probable that some elements of the crucifixion narrative in the *Gospel of Peter* developed from an independent tradition, but the miraculous elements and additions of details are mostly symptoms of the typical augmentation of tradition.[43]

3.4 Christology of Early Christian Literature

It is not our intention to provide here a survey of the theologies represented in Christian literature of the first three generations. If we did, this would be a voluminous book—albeit a fascinating testimony about a dialogue and spiritual struggle evoked by one constitutive event that all the participants tried to express in the most appropriate way. For our purposes, we shall only discuss some of the Early Christian literary units with regard to their

general christological intent—as models of the development of
Christologies and as documents that are possibly able to shed
more light on the first period of integration.

3.4.1 The Apostle Paul

Paul developed his Christology on the basis of older Christian
confessions, be it the Formula of Faith in 1 Cor 15:3b–5 (see
§1.2) or the formula of the Son in Rom 1:3–4 (see §3.1.4). He
found in them appropriate expressions of his experience with
the risen Lord (Gal 1:15–16; 1 Cor 9:1; 15:8). These are confessions proclaiming Jesus' resurrection in an apocalyptic sense
(see 1 Thess 1:10; cf. §3.2.1 and §3.2.2) and statements proclaiming the sacrificial power of his death (1 Cor 11:23–26),
often combining both, as in the Formula of Faith or in Rom
4:24–25: ". . . [Jesus, our Lord] was handed over to death for
our trespasses and was raised for our justification" (NRSV).

Paul's teaching on justification through Jesus' sacrificial
death on the cross was intended to be a new interpretation of
older confessions. Some scholars have judged it to be only a
"secondary crater" in his teaching—a theory designed so that
Paul could avoid certain problems in his missionary activity.[44]
But since it plays a decisive role not only in Galatians, but above
all in Romans, where Paul tried to offer a survey of his teaching
and proclamation (cf. 1 Cor 4:3–5; 2 Cor 5:10–21; Phil 1:11;
3:9), we must consider his teaching on justification to be a fun-
damental component of Paul's theology. Its logic is as follows.
Since God has raised from the dead just Jesus, as the one who
"hanged on a tree" and should have been cursed by God (Gal
3:13; cf. Deut 21:23), it must be Jesus who is the revelation of
God's strategy of saving the sinful and alienated humans, higher
than that which has been revealed through the Law. And since,
in the apocalyptic context, salvation means to acquit the
charged person of the punishment, i.e., to justify him, it is justification by which humans are saved from eternal death (Rom
3:21ff.). The only condition for being justified is to accept the
justification in its deepest nature, i.e., as grace.

Pauline teaching on justification was, incidentally, an important step toward reinterpretation of the apocalyptic dimension of the Christology of resurrection. The stress has shifted
from Jesus as the risen Lord, who was opening the new age, the

coming of which was expected in the very near future (1 Thess 1:10), to Jesus as the redeemer. His resurrection confirms that his sacrifice was accepted by God, so that all humans have the opportunity to reach their salvation.

The motif of salvation from grace may be better evidenced in Qumran than in Pharisaic teachings. In 1QS 11:9–15 or 1 QH 12:30–31, the author expressed his dependence upon God's grace in a way which can be considered a prototype of Pauline theology.[45]

According to Paul, such grace is accepted in faith as total confidence in God, as it is expressed especially in Gal 3:6 – 4:7 and Rom 3:21–26. The immediate consequence of accepting justification as grace is to wish this salvation for other people, too—for sinners, non-Jews, and even adversaries (Romans 12–13). These are features of Pauline Christology that cannot be explained from Qumran parallels and have their analogy in Jesus traditions. Another striking difference is that, for Paul, God's grace excluded the Law as a way to salvation, whereas, in Qumran, a strict obedience to the Law was expected—grace only filled the gaps.

Paul's statement on justification through faith and by the grace of God was provoked by the conflict in Antioch. The Christians who were pagans before they believed in Jesus as their Savior were considered second-class Christians by several Christian Jews (Gal 2:11ff.). Only Israel was considered to be the messianic people in Jewish expectations (including the apocalyptic ones). Paul's argument was that Israel is God's people because it is the people of Abraham's descendants. This has to be interpreted spiritually (as we may see in Philo of Alexandria), i.e., as a community of those who share Abraham's faith. This is more important than fulfilling the individual commandments of the Law. This included circumcision, since circumcision was introduced only after God's promise was given to Abraham (this is a rabbinic argument) and he believed it (see Gal 3:6ff. and Romans 4). This means that a non-circumcised pagan who believed in Jesus Christ as Savior is a legitimate son of Abraham and a member of God's people.

This was a major transformation of the Christian movement. It evoked conflicts, as we may see especially in the letters of Paul to Galatians, 1–2 Corinthians and Philippians, and from comments like that in 2 Pet 3:15–16. However, after the fall of Jerusalem in 70 CE, the Pauline theology enabled Christians to constitute a new group identity as a new people of God (parallel to Israel) and to keep the Jewish Bible (later called the Old Testament among Christians) as a witness to the prehistory of Jesus Christ.

Paul integrated several Christologies, not in an eclectic way, but by original and deep reflection. In fact, he developed the two dimensions of resurrection Christology that we mentioned earlier (§3.2.1), and it was under the influence of Pauline theology that the Gospel developed into a literary subgenre.

Pauline Schools developed various dimensions of his Christology. In Colossians and Ephesians, the presence of salvation is stressed (Col 2:12–13).[46] In the Pastoral Epistles (Timothy and Titus), the "not yet" of the eschatological fulfillment was emphasized (2 Tim 2:18). The apocryphal *Acts of Paul and Thecla* represented the non-patriarchal stream, incorporating the miracle tradition and, in terms of genre, oriented toward Greek Romance.[47] It is this tradition of Pauline interpretation which continued in Gnosticism.[48]

3.4.2 The Gospel According to Mark

It was obviously the author of the Gospel of Mark (the first formally organized Gospel) who created the literary pattern of the Gospel—a typically Christian subgenre of Greek biography.

Mark's accomplishment was the integration of various traditions using resurrection Christology as the organizing principle. The gospel in Mark 1:1 is obviously the Christian oral proclamation, as it is in the Pauline letters and the earlier christological tradition.[49] At that time, people did not call "gospel" a literary genre, as we do. Rather, gospel was a metaphoric summary of the oral tradition on Jesus' resurrection (§1.2.2). If we compare the end of the Gospel of Mark (in the oldest manuscripts the last verse is 16:8), i.e., Mark 16:6–7, with the Formula of Faith in 1 Cor 15:3b–5, we find striking parallels (see §1.2.1). Mark's Gospel culminates with the proclamation of Jesus' resurrection.

Several scholars considered that Mark 16:7 ("you will see him") related to the near **parousia**.[50] However, the Greek future tense is used as part of the narrative strategy, since the scene at Jesus' tomb is located between the resurrection and the appearances. From the reader's point of view, the attested appearances also belong to the past. If the appearances were identical with the universal revelation of Jesus' victory in the apocalyptic age to come, the relocation to Galilee (v. 7) would be meaningless.

Once the book culminated with the oral Gospel on Jesus' resurrection, all the other traditions were subsumed under this common denominator. Not only the Christology of resurrection and the Christology of sacrificial death are combined here, as in the Formula of Faith (§1.2.5), but also the apocalyptical Son of Man Christology culminating in the trial of Jesus within the passion narrative, as well as the divine man imagery in the miracle stories, which were obviously taken from popular Christian tradition. Within the Markan frame, the miraculous healings of Jesus become preliminary signs of the final, eschatological abandonment of suffering and death—fascinating symbols of resistance to persecution in the name of Jesus Christ.[51]

In order that the reader's attention may concentrate on the good news about resurrection, the christological elements of earlier units of oral tradition were suppressed through Jesus' repeated orders not to reveal his real identity, i.e., "until the Son of Man has risen from the dead" (9:9; cf. 1:25, 34, 44; 3:12; 5.43; 7:36; 8:26, 30). Some of the orders of silence are older and their original function was different, but, within the present text of Mark, most of them serve as stabilizers keeping the manifold tradition concentrated on the Gospel at the end of the book (the so-called messianic secret). The open ending of Mark supposes the liturgical participation of the confessing Christian community.

The title Son of God for Jesus also serves as a means of literary and theological composition culminating in the message about the resurrection of the crucified Jesus: In 1:11, the reader is initiated into the secret of Jesus. It is only he or she who knows who Jesus is (except for Jesus and God himself, of course). Jesus' contemporaries do not yet know it and their way toward understanding is the way toward Easter faith and Easter confession. Reading this, Christians may have learned their own way of life toward an authentic Christian confession. In 9:7 (The Transfiguration), three of Jesus' disciples are told of their master's real identity, but until his death on the cross, we do not hear any human confession of Jesus as the Son of God. Finally, in 15:39, it is the pagan centurion who pronounces the confession of Jesus as the Son of God (cf. Rom 10:9!). Originally, this statement may have been an expression of Hellenistic piety respecting heroic personalities; but, in Mark's interpretation, this is the apex of God's leading humans to understand what it means that Jesus is the very Son of God.

Mark's concept of his book as a biography culminating with Jesus' death and with the message on resurrection had far-reaching consequences. A carefully selected set of Jesus' sayings (about one-third of the text) was included. Before Mark, the Easter proclamation had shed new light on Jesus' sayings; their authority was enhanced by the fact of the risen Lord. But, according to Mark, it was not possible to generate any new sayings deriving their authority by Jesus as Lord. They belonged to the earthly life of Jesus. Thus, the sayings were conserved in a historical setting and protected against uncontrolled developments and reinterpretations. Their new application was possible only in an indirect way, through interpretation, through creation of subsequent texts (sermons, commentaries, meditations) that were expressly dependent on the basic text, which was firmly rooted in Jesus' time and historical setting. Here are the indirect beginnings of the idea of a Christian canon of Scriptures as a counterpart of the Jewish Bible.

In mainstream Christianity, the Gospel as genre prevailed and supplanted the other, earlier genres, especially the anthologies of Jesus' sayings. It is very difficult to say why Mark did not use the Q source. Was it because he did not know it? Or did he disagree with its theology? (Was it because of Q's love of enemies?—perhaps why the fourth Gospel does not mention it.) Or did he just think it unnecessary because Q was already rooted in the liturgy and teaching. These possibilities do not exclude each other, although it does seem improbable that Mark did not know of Q at all, since his Gospel is heavily influenced by Pauline theology and Paul did know of an orally transmitted set of Jesus' sayings, including the absolute love command (Rom

12:17–21). However, Paul's interpretation of the command and of the traditions associated with it, which we read in Rom 12:21 ("Do not be overcome by evil but overcome evil with good,"[RSV]) may be a reaction against possible misinterpretation. We have already mentioned that Luke and Matthew knew both Mark and Q, so it is very probable that these two texts were not considered alternatives, but were regarded as complementary traditions. Mark did not intend to integrate all Christian traditions into his Christian setting. For instance, he definitely knew the Lord's Prayer (see 14:36), but he did not quote it in his Gospel. Nevertheless, this question is still unanswered.

It is not within the scope of this work to discuss the Christology of every Early Christian text, even such an interesting text as the Gospel of Matthew. However, we have to at least mention a few features of Lukan and Johannine Christology, since they are the subject of current debate and have been very important in the development of the Christian liturgical year (Luke) and in the development of Christian doctrine (John).

3.4.3 Lukan Christology

Luke represents a new period of theological reflection which immediately influenced the canonical process.

From the older Christologies, Luke developed especially the tradition that we could call the prophetic Christology (see §2.2). Jesus had the prophetic gift and suffered the fate of a prophet (Luke 13:33b). With this in mind, Luke developed the portrait of Jesus he learned from Q (6:22–23; 11:49; 13:34). Jesus was the messianic prophet promised in Deut 18:15, 18 (Acts 3:22–23; 7:37)—the prophet with whom the Righteous Teacher used to be identified. However, Jesus is above all the Savior (Luke 2:11) bringing salvation (Luke 2:30; Acts 28:28). The main intent of Lukan Christology is expressed through his narrative and by his interpretation of parables that he found in a special Lukan source.[52]

Luke's theology is highlighted in the parable of the Prodigal Son (Luke 15:11–32). The younger son squandered his property. He was humiliated and near death (15:17c). His situation can be characterized as alienation ("But when he came to himself . . ." v. 17a). He overcame his alienation when he had a vision of an alternative life which does not tend toward death—a life in his father's house with bread (of life) for all. The Eucharist is an anticipation of this (eternal) life (Acts 2:46; cf. 27:36–37), and the forgiveness of the father preceded the confession of the son, when he still was "far off" (Luke 15:20).

The open way to the merciful father—this is Luke's interpretation of what had earlier been expressed by statements about Jesus' substitutive death. Twice the statement appears that the younger son was dead and is now alive (Luke 15:24 and 32). Luke obviously intended the parable to convey a new interpretation of what it means to die and be raised from death with Jesus Christ in baptism (Rom 6:1–11).

The older brother, who never disobeyed his father's commands (v. 29), was upset by his father's joy over the return of the younger son. The older one did not understand the terrible suffering of his sinful brother, who had lived in hunger and in the shadow of death. However, the father was consequential in his grace and forgiveness with both of his sons: ". . . all that is mine is yours" was his answer to the older son.

There is not much Christology in this parable. In Luke, salvation is primarily a matter of theology. Jesus is present only as the teller of the parable. Nevertheless, the teller was also the guarantor and witness. Jesus' salvific activity consisted in his being the representative of God, the father, who opens his house to sinners, to the alienated, and even to those living in a pagan setting. He not only represented God as the merciful father, but he also sealed this image of God with his life. By his resurrection, God vindicated him and confirmed his proclamation. According to Luke, resurrection meant that Jesus' image of God as the merciful father is true. And since all people are children of God (Acts 17:28), salvation is open for all.

This was a fascinating Christology, understandable for pagans who had no firsthand experience of the function of sacrifices in Israel. Jesus was the unique representative of the merciful God, the father of all humans. This is well understandable even in the twentieth century.

Nevertheless, Lukan Christology brought about some problems. For example, since the resurrection of Jesus was his vindication and Luke interpreted it as a kind of reanimation, it was necessary to introduce Jesus' ascension as his exaltation (in the older traditions, exaltation was identical with resurrection). Luke's image of Jesus as the prophetic Savior is associated with several heroic features which tend to relativize the depth of Jesus' suffering. For instance, on the cross there is no plaintive cry of abandonment; instead, Jesus dies in full control of the situation with the valiant words, "Father, into your hands I commend my spirit" (Luke 23:46). On the other hand, Luke was able to depict God's solidarity with suffering humankind and the kingdom of God as a promise for all alienated humans such that what is now called incarnation could be readily understood.

3.4.4 The Christology of the Johannine Writings

The Christology of the fourth Gospel is strikingly different from that of the Synoptics. The Johannine Jesus seems to be a divine being walking on earth—so he was characterized by Käsemann in 1966. His "I am's" (e.g., "the resurrection and life") are expressions of a Christology which presents Jesus as the exalted Lord who appears to believers. According to this Christology, Jesus seems to be a personal, but also a cosmic, Savior.[53] Believers experienced him as their personal counterpart, as their "you." As such he approached them from his own initiative, as the one who introduces himself as "I."

The "I am" as self-introduction of a deity was well known in antiquity,[54] even in the Old Testament (Exod 3:14; 20:2). Other parallels can be found in the *Odes of Solomon* (17:1, 16) and especially in the tractate called *Trimorphic Protennoia* from the Nag Hammadi texts.[55] This may be a text that was originally non-Christian, but was adapted into the present christianized shape before 200 CE. In any case, it illustrates the function of the "I am" sayings as means of revelation. Revelation is an insight into God's general intent or into his character, given in a special moment.

The "I am" sayings occur also in the Synoptic Gospels (Mark 6:50; 14:62). From the Revelation of John, we may deduce that some of them were formulated by Christian prophets who interpreted and applied the tradition in a creative way.[56]

In John, as well as in the *Trimorphic Protennoia* from Nag Hammadi, the general category is God's Word (John 1:1ff.; *Trim. Prot.* 47:15ff.). God has been revealed as the one who communicates with humans. Some portions from Qumran hymns are also representative of this revelatory genre.[57]

The christological dimension of Christian revelation is expressed by a paradoxical identification of the Word with the earthly existence of Jesus (John 1:14). The last "I am" in John 18:5–8 (delivered three times!) is, surprisingly, a confirmation of the earthly identity of Jesus of Nazareth. According to such a concept, the revelation happened not only in a special moment, but also through a concrete, earthly person. Resurrection Christology was thus interpreted in a new, non-apocalyptic way. It is no doubt significant that this reinterpretation was introduced in a time marked by the definitive split of Church and Synagogue.

Admittedly, this is not a full portrait of Johannine Christology, only a sketch of some of its features and tendencies. The methods of literary analysis enable us to see Johannine Christology, which appears speculative and **docetic,** in a new light. It is not a secondary development, but an interpretation of Jesus' message in another literary form. What we have discovered is that the second stream of Christian tradition, similar to wisdom literature and tending somewhat toward Gnostic interpretation, is present in the Fourth Gospel in its fully developed form.

The first stage of this tradition consisted of collections of wisdom sayings. The second, represented, for example, by the *Gospel of Thomas*, included sayings introduced by a comment stressing the authority of the author ("These are secret words which the living Jesus spoke," *GosThom*, proem.). The third stage presented the most important sayings in the revelatory "I am" style.

However, the Fourth Gospel put this developed shape of the sayings tradition into a biographical frame which was most probably derived from Mark. The pioneering study of J. H. Charlesworth on the Fourth Gospel (1995) discovered its relation to the Thomas tradition (including the *Gospel of Thomas* and the *Book of Thomas the Contender*). The incorporation of this tradition into a biographic frame was a bold experiment. The spiritually explosive alternative tradition of a living, heavenly Jesus talking to people (see §3.3.2.1) has been tamed, but still preserved. The reader's impression is by no means that of Jesus being truly human. He appears as the heavenly Savior and revealer of God's will, present through the Holy Spirit in his congregation. But it is this revealer of the transcendent order who makes his disciples aware of his identity as Jesus of Nazareth. And the Holy Spirit, active to the present time among Jesus' followers, brings the earthly Jesus to the remembrance of his present congregation. Because of the complexity of its structure and reflection, the Fourth Gospel greatly affected the development of Christian dogmatics.

3.5 Christology of the Canon

The Christian Bible as an authoritative collection of Christian classics originated through three stages.

(1) The first was the origin of the material of which the Christian Bible consists, i.e., of the individual biblical books.

(2) The second was the period in which the idea of composing such a canon arose. This took place at the beginning of the second century and was by no means a self-evident solution. To combine the Jewish Bible with a group of Christian texts was not acceptable for Jews, and to accept the Jewish Bible as a part of Christian Bible was not easy for several non-Jewish Christian groups (for example, the mid-second century Marcionites). Originally, the Christian proclamation was considered the authentic interpretation of Jewish Scripture (Law and Prophets). The idea of the canon is a complex literary expression of Christian confession which associated God's revelation with a contingent part of history, namely with the story of Jesus.

(3) In the third period, the discussion concentrated on the limits—the borders—of canon. It was the logical consequence of the concept of a canon that it would not be an unlimited selection of the best texts, but, rather, a selection of the best of the earliest—of the written testimonies of the "apostolic" generation. The closed, limited shape of canon reflects the attested revelation of Jesus Christ as an event of the past that anticipates and opens the absolute future.

The Bible that Jesus knew, the Jewish Scripture (Tanakh), was accepted as the authentic pre-history of Christians, so that the Christian canon consisted of two parts: the Jewish Bible (later called the Old Testament) and the Christian part, the New Testament. The fact that the Bible is organized into two units reflects the statement of very early confessions: "according to the Scripture" (see §1.2.7). The New Testament is not considered to be the final part of the Old Testament; it is its counterpart.

In Qumran, Scripture also had canonical authority and discussion concentrated on the interpretation of Law. Some of the Qumran texts were undoubtedly considered to be authoritative interpretations of the Law or new parts of the hymnal (1QH). This applies especially to the well-preserved texts from cave 1. However, it is difficult to say whether they were considered a counterpart of Scripture, or only as commentaries, since a clear and authoritative confession did not exist.[58]

As the first part of the Christian Bible, the Jewish Bible participated in the advance of Christianity into the pagan world, and soon the Gnostics themselves commented on the canonized Christian texts.[59]

The development of the canon definitely supported the Christology which included a firm feedback in Jesus of Nazareth (Jesus who "came in flesh") and led to a definite rejection of the other stream of texts and traditions—the stream that was concentrated on Jesus as the spiritually present Savior (see §3.1.4 and §3.3.2.1). On the other hand, the canon preserved a variety of Christologies. From the Gospels, four were accepted, even though their authors obviously intended to replace the other Gospels. Not only Pauline epistles and writings of Paul's various successors, but also those of some of his later opponents were included, such as John the Theologian, the author of Revelation, or the author of the Epistle of James.

The limited canon, though tied to the time of Jesus, nevertheless claimed to be a testimony of God's unique revelation through which his general intent, his all-embracing grace, and the deepest structure of his creation may be discovered. However, this discovery was principally mediated by written testimonies of different genres, which became ever more obscure to readers through the centuries. The more the Bible was declared

the norm, the more urgent was the need of its continual interpretation by sermon, catechesis, meditation, commentary, and
monographs, including such books as this one.

Notes

(Refer to bibliography for complete citations.)

Chapter 1

1. 4Q491, frgm.11.
2. See M. Smith, in Charlesworth, 1992.
3. Holtz, 1991.
4. Published posthumously in 1778 together with his other "Fragments" by the famous playwright and librarian Gotthold E. Lessing.
5. Advocated especially by Richard Reitzenstein in several of his German monographs from the first three decades of this century and in the U.S. by C. H. Kraeling, *Anthropos and Son of Man*, 1927.
6. The most influential edition was the 2nd edition, which appeared in 1913.
7. *The Parables of the Kingdom*, 1935.
8. *New Testament and Mythology*, in German, 1941; *Jesus Christ and Mythology*, 1958.
9. *Trajectories Through Early Christianity*, 1970.
10. *Sociology of Jesus Movement*, 1977 (translated from German).
11. Holtz, 1991.
12. Robbins, 1996, p. 37.
13. Robbins, 1996, p. 237ff.
14. Sanders, 1985.
15. Käsemann, 1964 and Perrin, 1974.
16. So it is, e.g., with B. L. Mack's or G. Lüdemann's interpretation.

Chapter 2

1. Haufe, 1985.
2. See especially J. H. Charlesworth, 1982; Evans, 1995, p. 111.
3. Cf. N. Perrin, 1976, II.A–B.1; J. D. Crossan, 1973, ch. 12.
4. *The Origin of the World* = NHC II/5; 125.2.6; 127.10–15; The *Apocalypse of Adam* V/5; 82.19–20, etc.
5. Cf. 4Q246.2.
6. The *Second Apocalypse of James* NHC V/4; 56.4–5; cf. The *Book of Thomas* NHC II/7; 145.15.
7. J. M. Robinson, in Robinson and Koester, 1971, ch. 3.
8. 1QM 12:15–18.

9. See J. D. G. Dunn, ch. 9, in Charlesworth, 1992/1; Betz and Riesner, 1994, ch. 9.
10. Plato, *Meno* 71E (Socrates, however, does not share this maxim unconditionally); for other evidence see Luz, 1985, ad loc.
11. 1QM 9ff.; cf. 1QH 12:22.
12. 1QS 10:19–20; cf. 1:10; 9:21–22.
13. Guelich, 1982, ch. V.
14. 1QM 9:10–17; 13:12–14 (in connection with the "poor"), etc. See Charlesworth, 1992, ch. 1.
15. Log. 3, cf. 113.
16. Especially J. D. Crossan, *The Historical Jesus*; B. L. Mack, *A Myth of Innocence*; M. J. Borg, *Jesus in Contemporary Scholarship*.
17. See especially Kloppenborg, 1987; Meier, 1994.
18. NHC XIII/1.
19. Tuckett, 1996, ch. 8.
20. As in B. L. Mack (1988, ch. I/2) or M. J. Borg (1994, 86ff.).
21. BSanh 11a.
22. 1QS 8:15–16.
23. 1QpHab 2:2–3.
24. 1QS 1:3.
25. 1QH 13:18; 14:25; 18:6, 10, etc.
26. 4QMMT^e, frgm. 14, col. 2.1ff.
27. 1QH 16:4–11; Charlesworth, 1989.
28. CD 1:7b–13a.
29. 1QpHab 7:4–5; cf. Deut 33:10; Ezra 7:10.
30. 1QpHab.
31. 1QpHab 7:1–17.
32. 8:1–3; cf. 2:6ff.
33. CD 6:10–11.
34. CD 1:19–21; 1QpHab 9:9–12.
35. Eisenmann and Wise, 1992.
36. Thiering, 1992, p. 401.
37. For these identifications in an older generation of scholars see Rowley, 1957.
38. E.g., Luke does call him prophet, Luke 1:76.
39. See 1 Kings 11:29–39; Jer 19:1–13; 27:1–15; 32:1–15; Ezek 4:1 – 5:4; cf. Acts 11:27; see also Schürmann, 1994, I. A classic example is Hosea, an entire portion of whose life was a symbolic event (Hos 1–3).
40. Schürmann, 1994.
41. K. G. Kuhn, in Stendahl and Charlesworth, 1992/1.

42. A similar intention is attested for the baptist movements in *SibOr* 4:164–192 (end of the first century CE).
43. Charlesworth, 1985, appendix, ch. 4.
44. Lucian, *Incred.* 16. For the problem, see Theissen and Merz, 1997, §10.
45. Guelich, 1982, ch. VI, p. 262.
46. *1 Enoch* 71:17; *SibOr* 3.573ff., etc.
47. 1QS 5:8; CD 16.2–9, etc.
48. *Pirq* 1.1; 3.17 (14).
49. See Hengel, *Nachfolge*, ch. 1.
50. Contra E. P. Sanders, 1995.
51. Cf. Hübner, 1986, ch. V.5.
52. E. P. Sanders, 1995, ch. 9.
53. For v. 29 see the parallel in Mark 8:34–35; Q (Luke) 14:27; for v. 30, *GosThom* 90.
54. Cf. *SibOr* 5:298 about heaven as God's dwelling place.
55. 4QOrd 159a frgm. I.2:6ff.
56. Not always, see Hengel, 1992.
57. 1QS 9:11; 1QSa 2:10–14; CD 20:1, etc.; cf. K. G. Kuhn, in Stendahl and Charlesworth, 1992/1. For other evidence from Qumran, see Evans, 1995, p. 111.
58. The dating of 4 Ezra is late first century CE. Qumran fragment 4Q246 does not support the idea of the Son of Man messianism (J. D. G. Dunn, in Porter and Evans, 1997); it only confirms the eschatological character of the messianic age. The hope linked with the Son of Man confirms potential messianic expectation only; in Ps 110:4 the messianic Lord (not identical with God as the Lord) bears priestly features of a special kind—"according to the order of Melchizedek" (see §2.3.3). For the messianic figures, see Evans, 1995, II.XII.
59. *1 Enoch* 37–71, especially 47:4. Unfortunately, this part of *1 Enoch* is not demonstrably pre-Christian.
60. The fragment is 4Q285. See Eisenmann and Wise, 1992, p. 30–35.
61. So G. Vermes, J. Maier, O. Betz and R. Riesner, García Martínez and Trebolle Barrera.
62. Cf. Witherington, 1990, ch. 4.
63. Cf. Zechariah 3. Regarding parallels in the rabbinic literature see Evans, 1992, pp. 140–141.
64. Mrázek, 1990, ch. 3.
65. R. Eisler, S. G. F. Brandon and their later followers.
66. This has been stressed by Horseley, 1987.
67. *J Ta'anit* 68d. See also Collins, 1996.

68. Xenofon, *Anabasis* 3.1.43.
69. Cf. Beardslee, 1991, 25ff.

Chapter 3

1. Cf. Smith, 1990, 38.
2. E.g., J. D. M. Derrett, 1982.
3. 1QapGen 20:12, 14, 15. Also, in the Qumran Targum to Job (11Q10.24:7 = Job 34:12), the Hebrew *šadday* as a designation of God in Job 31:12 is replaced by *marā'*. According to J. A. Fitzmyer (1979), the Hebrew *'ădōnay* (Lord) in Ps 110:1 could have been pronounced in Aramaic as *mārī'y* (my Lord).
4. NHC II/2.
5. NHC II/7.
6. NHC III/5.
7. NHC II/3.
8. Papyrus Berolinensis; NHC III/1; IV/1.
9. Cod. Askewianus.
10. E.g., Downing, 1992.
11. Pokorný, 1987, 3.1.3.
12. *Anfänge*, 1964.
13. Cf. Justin, *Dial. c. Trypho*, 80.
14. NHC VIII/2; 134:9–13; see J. M. Robinson, 1982.
15. In Plato, sunshine is a metaphor for the idea of good, *Resp* 507e-509b.
16. Pokorný, 1987, §3.1.2.2.
17. Cf. Fuller, 1985, p. 108.
18. See also Longenecker, 1970, 63–64.
19. Especially F. Hahn, 1963, ch. 2.
20. 4Q flor 1:11 (= 4Q 174:3, 11).
21. 4Q 246 = *Apoc ar* = psDanA^a 1.9; 2.
22. See Fitzmyer, 1979, ch. 4.2, 4; Dunn in Porter and Evans, 1997; Theissen and Merz, 1997, §16.
23. See Neufeld, 1963.
24. A comprehensive collection of material and evaluation is being offered by The International Q Project, publishing the database for individual Q units in the series Documenta Q (Leuven: Peeters, since 1996).
25. Bergemann, 1993.
26. Koester, 1990.
27. Sato, 1988, ch. 5.
28. Kloppenborg, 1988, ch. 3; Piper, 1989; and many other scholars who have joined them in this regard.
29. Tuckett, 1996, 325ff.

30. This puts in question the Pharisaic concept of Law. For another opinion, see D. R. Catchpole, 1993.
31. *Apoc. Petr.*, NHC VII/3; 79.21–31.
32. Ibid, 74.13ff. See also 82.21–26.
33. *GosPhil*, NHC II/3; 52.6–15; see Koschorke, 1978, chapters II/C and IV/D.
34. Johnson, 1997.
35. NHC III/5.
36. *Corp. Herm.* 1.12–15 and parallels in Nag Hammadi texts dealing with the god Man and his lower counterpart, e.g., NHC II/4; 87:27ff.
37. On Schmidt, see Riches, 1993, ch.14.
38. E.g., most of the contributors to *The Passion in Mark*, published by W. H. Kelber, 1976. See also Burton L. Mack, 1988, ch. 9.
39. A. Collins, 1994.
40. Marion L. Soards, in Brown, 1994, appendix IX.
41. See Brown, 1994, 10 for further information.
42. Crossan, 1985.
43. Brown, 1987.
44. Eg., A. Schweitzer and J. D. G. Dunn.
45. Braun, I, 1966, ad loc.
46. See Pokorný, 1991.
47. Cf. MacDonald, 1983.
48. Pagels, 1975.
49. See also Mark 8:35; 10:29; 13:10; 14:9. Only in Mark 1:14–15 is the Gospel that of Jesus' proclamation.
50. E.g., E. Lohmeyer in the 1930s and N. Perrin in the 1970s.
51. Balabán, 1990.
52. On Lukan Christology, see Pokorný, 1998, ch. 4.
53. Moody Smith, 1987, part 3.8.
54. Apuleius, *metam.* 11.5; Plutarch, *de Iside 9*.
55. NHC XIII.1.
56. See, e.g., Rev 1:17; Boring, 1982, ch. 7.
57. 1Q H 4:27; 7, 12—J. L. Price, in Charlesworth, 1972.
58. See Brooke, in Porter and Evans, 1997.
59. Metzger, 1987, 2/IV.

Glossary of Technical Terms

Apocalyptic — Relating to the final cosmic cataclysmic events.

Diaspora — The community of Jews who lived outside of Judea.

Didactic — Having the nature of a teaching.

Docetic — Relating to Docetism, an Early Christian heresy which held that Christ only appeared to have a human body, suffer, and die.

Dogmatics — The study of official church doctrine.

Ecclesiastical — Relating to the established church.

Eschatological — Relating to end times.

Eschaton — The end time.

Euaggelion — Greek, pronounced "you-ahn-gáy-leon," gospel, good news. *Eu* = good, *aggelion* = news, message.

Excursus — A brief discussion which departs from the main line of argument.

Exegetes — People who study Scripture to determine its inherent meaning without attempting to read their own ideas into it (*eisegeses*).

Hermeneutics — The study of the methodological principles for interpreting Scripture.

Kerygma — An apostolic proclamation about salvation.

Lexical — Relating to the use of words.

Liturgical — Relating to public worship.

Myth — Scholars use the word *myth* in its classical sense, as a term for a story about god(s), without the popular connotation of something which is not true. See the excursus on the function of myth which follows §1.2.5.

Origen — An Alexandrian (Egypt) Bible scholar and theologian of the third century CE (185–253/254).

Parousia — The second coming of Christ.

Pedagogical — Relating to teaching or education.

Pericope — A self-contained passage of Scripture.

Polemic — A vigorous, sometimes vicious, attack on other opinions.

Prognostics — Forecasts of the future.

Protology — The opposite of eschatology, relating to pre-existence (before creation).

Q — Abbreviation (allegedly for German *Quelle,* "source"), referring to a document containing a list of the sayings of Jesus which has not been discovered, but which is hypothesized based on the fact that there is common material in Matthew and Luke which does not appear in Mark. The theory is that Matthew and Luke referred to Q and Mark when writing their Gospels. See §3.1.3.

Soteriological — Relating to salvation.

Synoptic — From the Greek words for "with" and "see." Refers to the Gospels of Matthew, Mark, and Luke, which have much material in common and can be read side-by-side.

Bibliography

Balabán, M. "Faith or Fate" (Czech with German summary). In *The State and the Perspectives of Religious Studies in Czechoslovakia*. Brno: Society for Studies in Religion, 1990.

Bauer, W. *Rechtgläubigkeit und Ketzerei*. BHT 10. Tübingen: Mohr-Siebeck, 1934.

Beardslee, W. A. *Margins of Belonging*. Essays of the New Testament and Theology. Atlanta: Scholars, 1991.

Beasley-Murray, G. G. *Jesus and the Kingdom of God*. Exeter: Paternoster, 1986.

Bergemann, Th. *Q auf dem Prüfstand*. FRLANT 158. Göttingen: Vandenhoeck & Ruprecht, 1993.

Berger, K. *Theologiegeschichte des Urchristentums*. Tübingen: Francke, 1994.

Betz, O. and R. Riesner. *Jesus, Qumran und der Vatikan*. Freiburg and Basel: Brunnen Verlag Giessen, 1994.

Beyer, K. *Die aramäischen Texte vom toten Meer*. Göttingen: Vandenhoeck & Ruprecht, 1984.

Borg, M. J. *Jesus in Contemporary Scholarship*. Valley Forge, PA: Trinity, 1994.

Boring, M. E. *Sayings of the Risen Jesus*. SNTSMS 46. Cambridge: Cambridge University Press, 1982.

Boring, M. E., K. Berger and C. Colpe. *Hellenistic Commentary to the New Testament*. Nashville: Abingdon, 1995.

Bousset, W. *Kyrios Christos*. 5th ed. Göttingen: Vandenhoeck & Ruprecht, 1965.

Braun, H. *Qumran und das Neue Testament*. 2 vols. Tübingen: Mohr-Siebeck, 1966.

Brown, R. E. "The *Gospel of Peter* and the Canonical Gospel Priority." *NTS* 33 (1987): 321–343.

_____. *The Death of the Messiah*. 2 vols. New York: Doubleday, 1994.

Catchpole, D. R. *The Quest for Q*. Edinburgh: T.& T. Clark, 1993.

Charlesworth, J. H., ed. *John and Qumran*. London: Chapman, 1972.

_____. "The Concept of the Messiah in the Pseudepigrapha." ANRW II.19.10 (1979): 188–218.

_____. "The Historical Jesus in Light of Writings Contemporaneous with Him." ANRW II.25.1 (1982): 451–476.

_____. *The Discovery of a Dead Sea Scroll (4Q Therapeia).* Lubbock, TX: ICASALS, 1985.

_____. *Jesus Within Judaism.* AncB Ref Lib. New York: Doubleday, 1988.

_____, ed. *Jesus' Jewishness.* Philadelphia: Interfaith Institute, 1991.

_____, ed. *Jesus and the Dead Sea Scrolls.* AncB Ref Lib. New York: Doubleday, 1992.

_____. "An Allegorical and Autobiographical Poem by the Moreh Has-Sedeq (1QH8:4–11)." In *Sha'arei Talmon*, FS S. Talmon, eds. M. Fishbane and E. Tov, with W. W. Fields, pp. 295–307. Winona Lake, IN: Eisenbrauns, 1992.

_____, ed. *The Dead Sea Scrolls. Hebrew, Aramaic, and Greek Text with English Translations.* Tübingen: Mohr-Siebeck, and Louisville: Westminster-John Knox, 1994–.

_____. *The Beloved Disciple.* Valley Forge, PA: Trinity, 1995.

Chmiel, J. "Christianity and Qumran." *The Qumran Chronicle* 5 (1995): 46–54.

Collins, A. Y. "From the Noble Death to Crucified Messiah." *NTS* 40 (1994): 481–503.

Collins, J. J. "Jesus and the Messiahs of Israel." In *Geschichte-Tradition-Reflexion,* FS M. Hengel, III, pp. 281–302. Tübingen: Mohr-Siebeck, 1996.

Crossan J. D. *In Parables: The Challenge of the Historical Jesus.* New York: Harper & Row, 1973.

_____. *Four Other Gospels.* Minneapolis: Fortress, 1985.

_____. *The Historical Jesus.* San Francisco: HarperCollins, 1991.

Dahl, N. A. *The Historical Origins of Christological Doctrine.* Minneapolis: Fortress, 1991.

Downing, F. G. *Cynics and Christian Origins.* Edinburgh: T.& T. Clark, 1992.

Dunn, J. D. G. *Christology in the Making.* 2nd ed. London: SCM, 1989.

Ebeling, G. "Jesus und Glaube." In *Wort und Glaube.* 2nd ed. Tübingen: Mohr-Siebeck, 1962.

Eisenmann, R. H. and M. Wise. *The Dead Sea Scrolls Uncovered.*
  Shaftesbury: Element Books, 1992.

Evans, C. A. *Noncanonical Writings and New Testament Interpretation.* Peabody, MA: Hendrickson, 1992.

_____. *Jesus and His Contemporaries.* AGJU 25. Leiden:
  Brill, 1995.

Fitzmyer, J. A. *A Wandering Aramean.* SBLMS 25. Missoula, MT:
  Scholars, 1979.

Fuller, R. "The Theology of Jesus or Christology? An Evaluation of
  the Recent Discussion." *Semeia* 30 (1985): 105–116.

García Martínez, F. *The Dead Sea Scrolls Translated.* Leiden: Brill,
  1994.

García Martínez, F. and J. Trebolle Barrera. *The People of the Dead
  Sea Scrolls.* Leiden: Brill, 1995.

Gnilka, J. *Jesus von Nazareth.* HKNTSupl 3, Freiburg: Herder,
  1990.

Gray, J. *The Biblical Doctrine of the Reign of God.* Edinburgh: T.&
  T. Clark, 1979.

Guelich, B. *The Sermon on the Mount.* Waco, TX: Word Books,
  1982.

Hahn, F. *Christologische Hoheitstitel.* Göttingen: Vandenhoeck &
  Ruprecht, 1963.

Hare, D. R. *A. Son of Man Tradition.* Minneapolis: Augsburg-
  Fortress, 1990.

Haufe, G. "Der Reich Gottes bei Paulus und in der Jesustradition."
  NTS 31 (1985): 467–72.

Hengel, M. *Nachfolge und Charisma.* BZNW 34. Berlin: Töpel-
  mann, 1968.

_____. *The Charismatic Leader and his Followers.* TG. Edin-
  burgh: T.& T. Clark, 1981.

_____. *Between Jesus and Paul.* London: SCM, 1983.

_____. "Jesus, der Messias Israels." In *Messiah and Christos,*
  FS D. Flusser. TSAJ 32. Tübingen: Mohr-Siebeck,
  1992.

Holtz, T. "Überlegungen zur Geschichte des Urchristentums"
  (1975). In *Geschichte und Theologie des Urchristentums.* WUNT 57. Tübingen: Mohr-Siebeck, 1991.

Horseley, R. *Jesus and the Spiral of Violence.* Minneapolis: Fortress,
  1987 (paperback edition, 1992).

Hübner, H. *Das Gesetz in der synoptischen Tradition.* 2nd ed.
    Göttingen: Vandenhoeck & Ruprecht, 1986.

Jeremias. J. *Neutestamentliche Theologie I.* Gütersloh: G. Mohn, 1971.

Johnson, L. T. *The Real Jesus: The Misguided Quest for the Histori-
    cal Jesus and the Truth of the Traditional Gospels.* San
    Francisco: Harper, 1997.

Käsemann, E. "Anfänge christlicher Theologie, zuletzt." In *Exe-
    getische Versuche und Besinnungen II,* pp. 105–131.
    Göttingen: Vandenhoeck & Ruprecht, 1964.

_____. *Jesu letzter Wille nach Johannes 17.* Tübingen:
    Mohr-Siebeck, 1966.

Keck, L. E. *A Future for the Historical Jesus.* London: SCM, 1972.

Kloppenborg, J. S. *The Formation of Q.* Studies in Antiquity and
    Christianity. Philadelphia: Fortress, 1987.

Koester, H. *Ancient Christian Gospels: Their History and Develop-
    ment.* London: SCM, and Philadelphia: Trinity, 1990.

Koschorke, K. *Die Polemik der Gnostiker gegen das kirchliche Chris-
    tentum.* NHS 12. Leiden: Brill, 1978.

Landman, L., ed. *Messianism in the Talmudic Era.* New York:
    KTAV, 1979.

Longenecker, R. *The Christology of Early Jewish Christianity.* SBT
    17. London: SCM, 1970.

Lüdemann, G. *Die Auferstehung Jesu.* Göttingen: Vandenhoeck &
    Ruprecht, 1994.

Luz, U. *Das Evangelium nach Matthäus.* Teilband 1. *Mt 1–7.* EKK
    I/1. Zurich: Neukirchen-Vluyn, 1985.

MacDonald, D. R. *The Legend and the Apostle: The Battle for Paul
    in Story and Canon.* Philadelphia: Fortress, 1983.

Macgregor, G. H. C. "The Growth of the Resurrection Faith."
    ExpTim 50 (1988): 217–220, 280–283.

Mack, B. L. *The Myth of Innocence: Mark and Christian Origins.*
    Philadelphia: Fortress, 1988.

_____. *The Lost Gospel: The Book of Q & Christian Origins.*
    London: Harper-Collins, 1994.

Maier, J. *Die Qumran-Essener: Die Texte vom Toten Meer I-II.* UTB.
    München: Reinhardt, 1995.

Meier, J. P. *A Marginal Jew: Rethinking the Historical Jesus.* 2 vols.
    AncB Ref Lib. New York: Doubleday, 1991, 1994.

Metzger, B. M. *The Canon of the New Testament*. Oxford: Claren-
    don, 1987.

Moody-Smith, D. *Johannine Christology*. Edinburgh: T.&.T Clark,
    1987.

Mrázek, J. "Transformations of Messianism in the Aramaic Texts
    from Qumran" (in Czech). Diss. Prague, 1990.

Murphy-O'Connor, J., ed. *Paul and Qumran*. London: SCM Lon-
    don, 1968.

Neill, S. *The Interpretation of the New Testament, 1861–1961*.
    Oxford: Oxford University, 1966.

Neufeld, V. H. *The Earliest Christian Confession*. NTTS. Leiden:
    Brill, 1963.

Oegema, G. S. *Der Gesalbte und sein Volk: Untersuchungen messian-
    ischer Erwartungen*. SIJDZ. Göttingen: Vandenhoeck
    & Ruprecht, 1994.

Paffenroth, K. *The Story of Jesus According to L.* (JSNTSup 147),
    Sheffield: Sheffield Academic, 1997.

Pagels, E. *The Gnostic Paul: Gnostic Exegesis of the Pauline Letters*.
    Philadelphia: Fortress Press, 1975.

Perrin, N. *Rediscovering the Teaching of Jesus*. London: SCM, 1967.

_____. *The New Testament: An Introduction*. New York:
    Jovanovich, 1974.

_____. *Jesus and the Language of the Kingdom: Symbol and
    Metaphor in the New Testament Interpretation*. Phila-
    delphia: Fortress Press, 1976.

Pesch, R. *Das Markusevangelium I–II*. HTC. Freiburg: Herder,
    1976–1977.

Piper, R. A. *Wisdom in the Q Tradition: The Aphoristic Teaching of
    Jesus*. Cambridge: Cambridge University Press, 1989.

Pokorný, P. *The Genesis of Christology*. TG. Edinburgh: T.&T.
    Clark, 1987.

_____. *Colossians*. TG. Peabody, MA: Hendrickson, 1991.

_____. *Theologie der lukanischen Schriften*. FRLANT 174.
    Göttingen: Vandenhoeck & Ruprecht, 1998.

Porter, S. and C. A. Evans, eds. *The Scrolls and the Scriptures*.
    JSPSup 26. Sheffield: Sheffield Academic, 1997.

Riches, J. K. *A Century of New Testament Study*. Cambridge: Lut-
    terworth, 1993.

Ricoeur, P. *Liebe und Gerechtigkeit—Amour et justice*. Tübingen: Mohr-Siebeck, 1960.

Robbins, V. K. *The Tapestry of Early Christian Discourse*. London and New York: Routledge, 1996.

Robinson, J. M. "Jesus from Easter to Valentinus (or to Apostolic Creed)." *JBL* 101 (1982): 5–37.

Robinson, J. M. and H. Koester. *Trajectories Through Early Christianity*. Philadelphia: Fortress, 1970.

Roloff, J. "Das Markusevangelium als Geschichtsschreiben." *EvT* 27 (1969): 73–93.

Rowley, H. H. *The Dead Sea Scrolls and the New Testament*. London: SPCK, 1957.

Sanders, E. P. *Jesus and Judaism*. London: SCM, 1995.

Sato, M. *Q und die Prophetie*. WUNT II/29. Tübingen: Mohr-Siebeck, 1988.

Schürmann, H. *Jesus: Gestalt und Geheimnis*. Ed. by K. Scholtissek. Paderborn: Bonifatius, 1994.

Schweizer, Ed. *Jesus Christus I*. TRE XVI, pp. 670–726. Berlin and New York: de Gruyter, 1987.

Smith, J. Z. *Drudgery Divine: On the Comparison of the Early Christians and the Religions of Late-Antiquity*. Chicago: University of Chicago, 1990.

Stendahl, K. and J. H. Charlesworth, eds. *The Scrolls and the New Testament*. New York: Crossroad, 1992 (1st ed. 1957).

Theissen, G. and A. Merz. *Der historische Jesus*. 2nd ed. Göttingen: Vandenhoeck & Ruprecht, 1997.

Thiering, B. E. *Jesus and the Riddle of the Dead Sea Scrolls*. Garden City, NY: Doubleday, 1992.

Tuckett, Ch. M. *Q and the History of Early Christianity*. Edinburgh: T.& T. Clark, 1996.

Vermes, G. *The Dead Sea Scrolls*. London: Collins, 1977.

_____. *The Religion of Jesus the Jew*. London: SCM, 1993.

Vouga, F. *Geschichte des frühen Christentums*. UTB. Tübingen and Basel: Francke, 1994.

Witherington, B. III. *The Christology of Jesus*. Minneapolis: Fortress, 1990.

Wolff, Ch. *Der erste Brief des Paulus an die Korinther II*. THNT 7/3. Berlin: EVA, 1982.

About the Author

Petr Pokorný was born in Czechoslovakia in 1933. He holds an Mgr. (M.Div.) degree from the Comenius Faculty of Protestant Theology in Prague and a Ph.D. and a Dr.Sc. from Charles University. He has served as vicar and minister for two congregations of the Protestant Church of Czech Brethren. He has taught at the Comenius Faculty, the University of Greifswald, and is currently professor, director of the Biblical Institute and head of the faculty at the Charles University Protestant Faculty of Theology. He has been a visiting professor or substitute at Pittsburgh Theological Seminary, Princeton Theological Seminary, and the University of Tübingen and has presented visiting lectures at more than thirty universities in Europe and the United States.

In 1978, he participated in the third Nag Hammadi expedition. In 1988, he participated in excavations in Jordan with the German Protestant Institute for the Archeology of the Holy Land. He is a member and past president of Studiorum Novi Testamenti Societas, and past chairman of the Scholarly Forum of the United Bible Societies for Europe and the Middle East. He is now a consultant to the Committee for the Russian Literary Bible Translation and a corresponding member of the Akademie der Wissenschaften zu Göttingen.

He has published sixteen books and over a hundred papers, articles, and reviews.

His wife, Vera, is a child psychologist. They have three daughters, one son, and seven grandchildren.